# BECOMING
# ELITE

## Nine Keys to Maximizing Your Potential

**Trevor Brown**

This book is dedicated to my beautiful wife, Jade,
and our two daughters, Brynnlee and Kinsley.
They are my reason for everything I do.

Published 2023 by Trevor Brown.

Print edition ISBN 979-8-9881307-0-3
Kindle edition ISBN 979-8-9881307-1-0
EPUB edition ISBN 979-8-9881307-2-7

Text is set in Alverata.

Cover design is copyright ©2023 by Copycat Printing, Kearney, Nebraska.
Editing and design by Karen Nelson Editing and Design, Bertrand, Nebraska.

# CONTENTS

"Strength does not come from physical capacity.
It comes from an indomitable will."

— Mahatma Gandhi

# FOREWORD

Gym owner.

Personal trainer.

Nutrition coach.

Mother.

Wife.

As I fulfill these roles, it is important that I exhibit the characteristics and values that can help my peers, clients, friends, and family become the best version of themselves. As the wife of Trevor Brown, I share several of my roles with him. He has helped establish and develop habits within the spouse, parent, and co-worker relationships we foster together. In *Becoming Elite*, it is evident how Trevor became a successful entrepreneur: He practices what he preaches. His passion, charisma, and leadership make him admirable to anyone he interacts with, enabling him to positively impact others' lives.

I met Trevor at the grand opening of his gym when it was in an old automotive shop. He made a big impression on me. He was the first one in the door by 6 a.m. and the last one out at 8 p.m. every day. He always kept the gym clean and orderly; if it wasn't, he would stay later or arrive early to make sure it was. His phone constantly rang, and he'd answer every single phone call. I was in awe — and still am today — of how he spoke so confidently and made a friendship during every phone call. His life revolved around his gym and, most importantly, his members who became friends. He invested in people's lives and wanted them to succeed with their goals and leading a healthy lifestyle. Since Day One, it has always been about the people and relationships. Hanging out with the members late at night after the last class of the day, or on the weekends for football parties, was the norm — something that helps cultivate the culture and environment of the gym today.

Trevor is the light of each day. He's always smiling. He's the first person to say hello and ask you how your day is. He's got high energy and a positive vibe, and he's a smooth jokester. No matter what situations he has going on behind the scenes, he is consistent with how he acts. As his wife, I get to see a different side compared to what most people see, but honestly, it doesn't change much. There were, are, and will be hard times, yet Trevor has the demeanor and tenacity to handle those in a professional and calm manner.

When his partner walked out on him the day his new gym opened, I could never have deduced from his demeanor how much that affected him. Yes, we communicated, and he informed me of the struggles he knew were ahead, but it appeared he had everything under control, and his routine stayed consistent. I know now that there were many stressful situations and changes before everything worked out okay. It's how you react to situations that will determine your success or failure, but failure isn't in Trevor's vocabulary. When there is a will, there is a way, and that is 100% true of Trevor.

I grew up in a small town, played every sport, and was involved in many other extracurricular activities. I received a full-ride scholarship to play basketball at a Division II university where I became an All-American. It takes a lot of hard work and dedication at a young age and beyond to be successful. Even as I am thankful for every opportunity given to me during my journey to become a collegiate basketball player, I wish I'd had the experience Trevor is providing for the youth in our community. I would have had an additional advantage if I could have moved better athletically and in the weight room. My body would have been better prepared if I had known proper nutrition as a high school athlete, and my mind would have benefited from another opportunity for someone to instill values and characteristics to prepare me for life after my parents' house. College basketball quickly taught me that I needed more than just athletic ability. Actions, attitude, focus, effort, and habits make an individual successful. Additionally, you need to be prepared to take advantage of opportunities when they present themselves. As much as athletics were a significant part of my life, it was the characteristics developed through an organized environment that molded me into the adult I am today.

I hope you enjoy the experiences and life lessons Trevor presents in this book. They are reminders for adults on how to live our lives and instill good values in our children, and they provide youth a template for success. I am so thankful I have a selfless, caring husband who strives to be the best version of himself for his family and also for all the people he interacts with on a daily basis. So please, enjoy the words and take a peek inside the life of the man who leads our lives, while learning the nine keys to maximize your potential in *Becoming Elite*.

*Jade Brown*

# PREFACE

As I look back on my life so far, I find myself wondering how things would be different today if I would've known then what I know now. But as much as I wish I could change some decisions of the past, each one of those molded me into the person I am today. My trials, tribulations, failures, and successes provided the template for this book.

My biological father was an alcoholic who walked out when I was two years old. My mom remarried a few years later, and my stepdad provided a father-like presence in my life. They divorced when I was 18, and my relationship with my stepdad has faded over the years. My mom's unconditional love and support have afforded me the opportunities I have today. I remember my mom working 16-hour days. She would leave before we went to school and come home late at night. As I lay in bed at night, I would hear the garage door open and then yell for her to come see me as she walked in the door. That five minutes I got to see her before I fell asleep was the best time of my day.

It took me having kids to understand how hard it must've been for my mom to work so much and not be with my sister and me. Currently, I struggle with finding that balance. I want nothing more than to be with my kids all the time, but for now, to provide for my family, I must work long hours. There are things I could've done differently years ago that could have allowed me more time to be with them today. Those are things I want to share with you through this book.

I was 12 when I was introduced to weightlifting by my uncle. From an early age, I dreamed of someday playing professional baseball. School came easy to me, but discipline did not. My junior year of high school, I often cut class, forcing me to take extra classes my senior year to graduate. My ACT scores allowed me to walk on at the University of Nebraska at Kearney to play baseball. Again, a lack of discipline led to me dropping out of school to pursue a career in real estate with my mom.

Over the years, I did just enough to get by, never really putting my full effort into the real estate business. Always in the back of my mind was the idea of opening a gym. I would work out for hours each day. I read every bodybuilding magazine I could get my hands on and did extensive research on anything, and everything, related to health and fitness. It was my true passion.

In 2012, I opened Kearney CrossFit. My business partner walked out on me in 2013, and I had to scramble to keep things together. At that point, something changed in me. I knew that I had found what I loved doing, and I was going to do whatever it took to be successful. I committed everything I had to growing my business. I turned my attention to the people of our gym and away from myself. I decided to put my own workouts on the back burner and make our members my first priority, always.

From 2013 to 2017, the gym scraped by with no more than 120 members. I borrowed money multiple times, and my mom kicked in to help whenever needed — not because of a lack of effort on my part, but because it took a while to learn what I needed to do to grow. I read books and watched YouTube videos from highly successful people. I taught myself how to grow a business, develop people, and operate successfully. Beginning in 2017, we have developed an incredible youth program, and we also started a very successful nutrition business. In the five years from 2017 to 2022, we doubled our membership base and increased our revenue sixfold.

I say all of this with the utmost humility. Extensive amounts of hard work and some incredible people got me where I am today. A handful of our gym members also helped me in ways that I can never repay. They saw what we were trying to build, and they believed in me.

I have taken more than a decade of business practice and a lifetime of experiences and put it all together in one place. This book will provide you with a template for how to maximize your potential in all areas of your life.

Remember this: When you find something you love to do, put every ounce of your energy into it. There are no shortcuts. Unmatched hard work and discipline are the things that will make you successful. Combine that with a genuine passion for positively impacting others, and you will do incredible things with your life.

# INTRODUCTION

This book was written as a guide to help young people build a foundation for success. However, the nine keys to maximizing potential are applicable to people of all ages. These are the lessons I will teach my children as they grow up and the ones I wish I had known earlier in life. I talk about these nine keys with my employees regularly, and my wife and I live by them. As you read this book, pay extra attention to *the words in italics*. These are things you should write down and refer to from time to time.

It's easy to get so caught up in attaining the goals we set that the magic of the journey is often lost. While dictionaries define success as "the accomplishment of a task or goal," I encourage you to look at it differently. Goals are good to have, and they can provide motivation and accountability, but achieving them shouldn't be the end all, be all. The things you learn while putting forth effort and working to reach your goals will far outweigh the achievement of the goals themselves.

For example, each year in any given sport, teams set out with an end goal in mind. For some teams, winning the championship is the goal. For others, simply having a record above .500 may be the goal. Finishing the season with a winning record is a goal that multiple teams will accomplish, but just one team each year can win the championship. Does that then mean that teams with losing records and those that didn't win the championship were unsuccessful? I would argue that the teams that fall short of winning the championship have every chance of being more successful.

Losing reveals far more about character than winning does. You cannot control what happens to you, but you can always control how you respond. A team might play their best game of the season and still lose, so building upon the things done well is critical moving forward. Is success in that game defined by the score or by the way in which the game was played? Choosing to define success solely by end results leaves no room for growth or self-improvement. Focusing on the positives and the things done well, while learning from mistakes, is what leads to long-term betterment.

With that in mind, as you read this book, write down your goals and set out to accomplish them with relentless energy. Simultaneously, realize that the friendships made and the lessons learned along the way are far more important than the goals themselves. Begin to define success by your actions and efforts rather than by the accomplishment of tasks.

Try to imagine yourself living out each scenario included in this book, and find ways in which each one applies to your life. It is one thing to read about a situation, and it is another to imagine yourself inside it. There are going to be things that jump out at you, and there will be some that seemingly don't apply at this point in your life. Put thought and effort into each chapter; you never know what your future holds. Each of the nine keys to success applies to anyone, of any age, from any walk of life.

CHAPTER 1

# ONE LIFE, ONE OPPORTUNITY

There are many things to remember as you navigate life. However, in my experience, there are nine things that stand out. Understanding these nine things is the key to unlocking your true potential. At the very top of this list is the fact that you have one life. You have one big opportunity to do as much with your life as possible!

It's not the opportunities you are presented with that make you elite. It's what you do with those opportunities that makes you elite.

In a 2021 interview with Peyton Manning, Tom Brady was asked what advice he would give to other players. Brady said that he tells all young players not to waste their opportunity when it comes. Even though he was the 199th pick in the NFL Draft, Brady got an opportunity, and he made the most of it. There were 198 players taken ahead of Brady, and thousands of others have stepped on an NFL field, so what makes him different? What makes Tom Brady one of the all-time greats? I believe the answer lies in his exceptional preparation and attention to detail.

The U.S. military, firemen, police, and doctors are trained to be prepared for any and every situation. We expect no less from these people. Imagine it's your house on fire, your family in a hostage situation, or you in a car crash; you would want the people responsible for your health and safety to be as prepared as possible. What if you are on an airplane and an engine goes out? Your life hangs in the balance, and in that moment it all comes down to the preparation and attention to detail of the pilot and flight crew. It's easy to see the need for these people to be so well-trained. Your life should be no different. Your success will ultimately be determined by your effort, hard work, preparation, and attention to detail.

The landscape of youth sports has changed drastically since I was a kid. I grew up playing baseball and loved every minute of being on the field. In Little League, we played 15 games in the regular season, and then some players were selected to the all-star team. If you didn't make the all-star team, your season was over. That team, however, progressed through Districts, State, and Regionals as long as it kept winning. I was fortunate enough to be a part of two teams that made it to Regionals, and I will never forget those experiences.

Today, there are more opportunities for kids than ever before. For example, there are numerous travel teams for all sports. Kids try out for these teams, and if they are cut, parents simply form another team. This process has led to the exponential growth of traveling youth sports across the country. Each team gets custom uniforms, has the best equipment, and stays in hotels. Many of these teams are traveling across state lines from the time kids are in grade school. This provides kids with amazing experiences and opportunities.

What is the drawback to all of this? The problem is that kids don't know what it's like to fail. They don't know what it's like to have a season cut short because they didn't make the all-star team. They never understand that they have to work hard and earn a spot on a team. They get all the gear and the swag, travel across the country, and are treated like pros without ever really having to work for it.

Parents have good intentions, and I suppose to some extent I will also provide these opportunities to my children. But as a kid growing up, it is important to know that life will not always hand you countless opportunities, and as parents providing these opportunities, it is important to remember that your kids need to earn them and they need to work to make the most of every opportunity they are given. Life is not full of handouts.

As kids get older, sports take a back seat to school and work. Students quickly learn the importance of studying for tests, completing assignments on time, and that effort really does make a difference. The most prepared people will get the best grades and move up the most quickly in the working world. Some people need to study more than others to achieve good grades. Some will need to spend extra time to complete tasks others can do easily. However, in the end, your preparation and attention to detail will determine your success. With all that in mind, what happens if we miss opportunities and aren't prepared?

Life is one big opportunity. It's a massive Choose Your Own Adventure® story for every person. Your actions directly affect your outcome more than anything else does. Once you choose one path, you don't get to go back in time and change your decision. That means you need to take advantage of every minute of every day, so that you are always headed down the path to success. That being said, just because you fail doesn't mean another opportunity won't present itself.

You get one shot at high school. Your study habits, grades, work ethic, and test scores are compounded year after year until you graduate. The effort you put in over the course of four years will largely determine the doors that are opened for you when you graduate. If you choose to slack off, not study, skip school, and prioritize other things during your high school career, many opportunities will never present themselves. Even as an athlete, your focus still needs to be school. Beyond that, the extra practices and hours in the gym or weight room will also open doors.

Too many kids figure out these concepts as seniors, or even after high school, and there is no going back. Ideally, every young person would develop positive habits from the time they are freshmen, work hard to set themselves up for success, and graduate with doors wide open. What happens if they don't? It's okay!

The awesome part about life is that opportunities are constantly popping up, and a person can even create more for themselves! The old saying is true: "When one door closes, another one opens." Life doesn't end at high school graduation. Many of the most successful people in the world today weren't A+ students. Don't dwell on the past. Learn from your experiences, and work hard to make sure you are ready when your opportunity comes.

This same concept applies to all areas of life. School, sports, work, and relationships all require effort, and the more we put in, the more successful we will be. We will all make mistakes along the way, but remember that life is one big opportunity comprised of many smaller ones. It's never too late to turn things around or to change your path.

When an opportunity comes, you will either rise to the occasion or you will fail. It's not luck. It's not about being the smartest, the most talented, or the first pick. It's about you and the work you put in leading up to that opportunity.

### Time truly does heal all.

Time. It is something we want to both slow down and speed up. It is also something we can't get back. In every difficult situation, there is also an opportunity to understand something new and find a new way forward.

Consider these situations:

1. Losing the championship game
2. The end of a relationship
3. Job loss
4. Bombing a test
5. Letting people down
6. The passing of a loved one

Just as you can't change the past, you can't press fast forward and skip over grief and heartache. Learning to deal with difficult times is part of growing and developing as a person.

Understand this about those situations:

1. There will be another game.
2. You will go on another date.

3. There are more jobs out there.
4. There will be other tests to take.
5. You will have the opportunity to lift others up.
6. You have memories to cherish.

Do this as you move forward:

1. Practice more. Study more film. Hit the gym harder.
2. Be better in relationships. Open your heart again.
3. Find your passion. Go apply for other jobs.
4. Study more. Seek out a tutor. Retake that test.
5. Learn from your mistakes. Be confident in your growth.
6. Celebrate and remember all the good times together.

Time. Remember, you can't get it back. You can't slow it down. You can't speed it up. You *can* make the most of it.

### Everyone has help along the way.

Understand that it's okay to ask for help. Also know that people want to help you. As a gym owner, I have had the privilege of helping thousands of people along the path to their health, fitness, and wellness goals. People come to me looking for guidance with nutrition, workouts, and life in general. Changing lives is one of the most rewarding parts of my job. I enjoy helping people, and it's what keeps me motivated on a daily basis. Messages from people telling me how much they appreciate my help, and from parents telling me how much of a positive influence the gym has been on their kids, make every long hour worth it.

Almost every professional athlete has at least one coach. Every one of them had a coach at some point along the way. Many hire private coaches to help them in the offseason. There are head coaches, position coaches, mental coaches, nutrition coaches, physical therapists, chiropractors, and financial advisors who all play a role in the lives of professional athletes. The more successful you are as an athlete, the more coaches you seem to have. With that in mind, why should the rest of us be any different? If money were no object, we should all have a team of coaches teaching us, guiding us, and leading us to success.

While we may not have the resources of a professional athlete, we do have tools at our disposal:

- Reading books is a great way to improve knowledge and better yourself.
- The internet can be a great resource as long as you choose credible sources. Use your smart phones for good. Watch videos from successful people. So much information is now at our fingertips. Take advantage of that!
- Seek out people who are where you want to be. Ask them what made them successful. Ask for advice. Ask to job shadow them. Most of them will be happy to share their experiences with you.

Whether it's because you are down on your luck or you simply want to better yourself, ask for help. If you don't ask, you won't get it. Always be gracious in return. Write a thank-you letter and give credit where credit is due. Say thank you.

### Nobody owes you anything.

The concept of "fair" does not apply in life. The sooner you understand this, the sooner you can move on and get to work. Everyone does not come from the same socio-economic background. Everyone is not born with the same physical attributes. No matter how hard I try, I will never be 6 feet, 3 inches and 240 pounds. Some people are naturally smarter than others. You cannot control the effort of others. Even if you outwork others, they may be rewarded equally or better than you are. There are many things you cannot control, but you can control your effort. You have the ability to be the very best version of you possible. I've seen more naturally talented people waste their genetic gifts than I can count. In my experience, more often than not, the people who did not hit the genetic lottery outwork those who did.

As a young person, realize that your parents do not have to pay for you to play travel sports. They do not have to buy you a car and name-brand clothes. They do not have to pay your way to college. They do not have to give you an allowance. If you are afforded those things, be gracious in return. Moreover, put forth every bit of effort you can so as not to waste the time, energy, and money your parents give to you.

As a parent, give your kids all you can. Love them and provide them with opportunities to the best of your ability. Teach them fiscal responsibility. Make them earn their opportunities. Do not simply hand them everything. Teach them that hard work is rewarded. More than anything, know that your *time* is more valuable than any amount of money.

## Be true to yourself.

People want to be accepted. They want to fit in. They want to be a part of a team. The sense of belonging, community, and camaraderie that comes from being part of something bigger than yourself cannot be equaled. The relationships forged through teams are lifelong. Being a part of a team means that you rely on others and, in turn, they rely on you. You need each other. A team will only be as strong as its weakest link.

These are all examples of teams:

1. You and a small group assigned to a school project
2. You and the coaches and athletes on a sports team
3. You and your significant other
4. Your family

At some point in your life, you will be a part of a team. For that team to endure and be successful, you will need to learn patience, sacrifice, and compassion for others. You will learn that the team is more important than any individual. A team shares highs and lows together. A team wins together, and it loses together. Nothing else offers the life lessons that come along with teamwork.

As important as teams and relationships are, never sacrifice your beliefs and values for anyone or any group of people. Do not change who you are to fit in. Your values are intrinsic to your way of life. At our gym we have a set of values that we instill in each of our coaches and preach to our members:

1. Be positive.
2. Control your effort.
3. Care about others.

All our coaches must live out these values on a daily basis. Without their buy-in, our community would not be as strong as it is. If a person does not align with our values, they will not even be considered as a potential coach. This starts at the top and trickles down to our members. A person who continually opposes our values is asked to leave. In a decade, I have only had to ask two people to leave the gym. I believe that our coaches have the opportunity and ability to positively change lives, and it is our job to do so. It starts with exhibiting these values personally, instilling these values in our members, and never wavering from them.

## Lead by example.

Great leaders set the tone by practicing what they preach. It is very difficult to earn the trust of those around you if they never see you doing the things you tell them to do. Not only will your example be a positive influence on those around you, but it will allow you to better understand the experiences of others.

I program all the workouts for our gym. Each day we do a different workout with the idea of building an all-inclusive, well-rounded fitness program. I also do the workouts I program. Why would I want our members to experience anything less than I want for myself? If my intentions are to create the best program for our community, then shouldn't I be doing it, too? Doing the workouts also allows me to make changes for the next day if a workout was easier or harder than I anticipated. I've been programming for every level of fitness and doing my own workouts for nearly two decades. Still, nothing replaces the experience of doing the workout myself. Additionally, when our members see me doing the workouts, it brings validity to the program. And sweating together and participating in classes alongside everyone else builds camaraderie.

As kids, we learn by watching our parents. For example, most parents tell their kids not to smoke and drink. Those words don't mean much if Dad brings home a six-pack of beer each night and Mom smokes a pack of cigarettes a day. A coach expects players to show up to practice on time. Being late individually has team consequences such as running laps. With a system like

*Becoming Elite*

this in place, athletes quickly learn not only to be on time but to show up early. What do you think would happen to the team dynamic if the coach were consistently late to practice?

No matter how successful you become, you are never above doing the little things you expect of those around you. On the long-running TV show "Undercover Boss," high-level executives and business owners go undercover and work in their own companies as ordinary employees to gain insight about their employees' experiences. By the end of each episode, the boss has gained a new appreciation for their employees. Leaders lead from the top, but sometimes taking a step down can be valuable in more than one way. Imagine how much respect employees would have for the CEO who mops the floors. If you want respect, don't be reluctant to mop the floors.

## Learn from your mistakes, and don't be afraid to fail.

If you want to maximize your potential, don't go into anything with the idea that you will settle for average. Hunter S. Thompson said, "Anything worth doing, is worth doing right." Set the bar high, and aim for perfection in everything you do. Once the bar is set, pour every ounce of your energy into reaching that target. If you reach your goal, awesome! If you don't, rest easy in the knowledge that you couldn't have done anything more at that time. I say "at that time," because you are going to make mistakes. No one walks through life without messing up along the way. Learning from those mistakes is what will allow you to improve your performance next time. Grab hold of the idea that you will not be perfect and there is absolutely nothing wrong with that. What will make you elite is what you choose to do with failure. Begin to look at failure as an opportunity and not a setback.

Mat Fraser won five individual CrossFit Games titles and has proven to be the fittest man in CrossFit history. Being the owner of a CrossFit gym, I have followed his career closely. One of the coolest stories about Fraser comes from him failing. In multiple interviews over the years, he has talked about how he handles failure. His approach is what sets him apart from everyone else in the world and ultimately led to his unmatched success in CrossFit.

*Becoming Elite*

In his first regional competition in 2013, Fraser finished fifth and missed going to the CrossFit Games. His downfall was his conditioning, specifically his performance on the rower. The next offseason, he rowed 5,000 meters every day to eliminate that weakness. In 2014, he finished in second place at the CrossFit Games to Rich Froning, who, at that time, was called the "fittest man in history." Fraser considered that year a success. Froning retired from individual competition, and Fraser was poised to take the title in 2015. Again, he finished in second place. He was in the lead going into the final workout, but a poor performance with handstand push-ups was his downfall that time. Fraser said he got complacent that year and didn't quite give 100% effort each day in his training. From that point forward, he never lost another in-person competition.

Even with all his success, he never lost his edge. In 2015, he had a subpar finish in a sprint event. That offseason he trained with a local high school track team to improve his running. As a professional athlete, he put his ego aside and ran alongside high school freshmen. In 2016, he took a first-place finish in the final heat of the sprint event on his way to his first title. I remember Fraser talking about the time his coach asked him to try a new rope climb technique. He was already proficient at rope climbs, but he tirelessly worked to perfect the new technique. In the end, he went back to his original way, but not after exhausting every effort to perfect the new one. This approach to failure is what made Fraser untouchable for so long.

On your path to success, you will make mistakes. You will fail more than once. Never failing doesn't make you great. It simply means you didn't set the bar high enough to begin with. Don't be afraid to take risks and make mistakes. Failure is not a sign of weakness. Rather, it is an opportunity for improvement.

### Dream big.

Over history, humankind's greatest accomplishments were once nothing but far-fetched dreams. Less than 100 years ago, a man first walked on the moon. One hundred years before that, cars had yet to be invented. Michael Jordan was once just a kid

*Becoming Elite*

hoping to make the varsity basketball team. Amazon started in a garage. A couple of college friends started Facebook. Without big dreams, we would still be riding horses, lighting our homes with candles, "calling" each other via Pony Express, and Air Jordan never would've taken flight.

Landing a man on the moon, running a sub-4-minute mile, building the Great Pyramids, harnessing electricity, building cars, and creating the internet are all examples of incredible accomplishments. Each one started as a dream, and before that they would've been impossible to even imagine. Someone had to break the status quo and dream big for these things to come to fruition.

No matter what it is, people are going to tell you it can't be done. The road to greatness is crowded with naysayers, littered with speedbumps, and clogged with roadblocks. It doesn't matter if you are driving, running, walking, or crawling down that road. Just keep pushing forward. Ninety-nine percent of people are going to give up before they realize their dreams. Do not let the shortfalls of others deter you. You do not have to be like everyone else. Your effort will determine your success. Only you decide when you quit!

You can have all the ambition, drive, and determination in the world, but you still need a plan. Start by writing down your goals. Then break down the steps needed to get there. Saying you're going to play college basketball, or that you'll be a successful business owner, is vague and overwhelming for most people. It is important to take the appropriate steps when designing a plan for success. Begin by defining your goal. Then, set measurable objectives. Finally, assign tasks that will help you meet your objectives.

These are some big concepts for a young person to grasp. Remember, nobody does this alone. Seek out advice from successful people and don't hesitate to ask for guidance along the way. Having a visual plan will bring it to life. Hold yourself accountable to your goals, and give 100% effort to seeing your plan through to the end. Only spend time with people who keep you on the road to greatness. Dream big and don't be afraid to chase those dreams!

## FINAL THOUGHTS

You get one chance at life, and you have one opportunity to chase your dreams. Define your goals and make a plan to reach them. Decide the type of person you want to be, and stay true to yourself along the way. Accept failure as an opportunity for growth, and always dream big.

## REFLECTION

1. What opportunities do you have in front of you now?
2. How can you make better use of your time?
3. Who is someone you can ask for help with your goals?
4. What values are most important to you?
5. When is a time you or someone you know led by example?
6. When have you failed, and how did you respond?
7. What are your dreams?

CHAPTER 2

# THE COMPANY YOU KEEP

Your character reflects the character of the few people you spend the most time with. If you spend your time with successful, driven, motivated people, you will find it very difficult to be lazy and unproductive. The opposite also holds true. If you hang around unambitious, negative people, you will find it difficult to be optimistic, motivated, and successful.

Write down, remember, and frequently refer to your goals. Look at those, and think about what kind of people you need in your life to be successful. Remove the people from your life who won't help you get there. Making the decision to do so will be difficult and rewarding at the same time.

Imagine this scenario: You are part of a collegiate sports team, entering as a freshman. You are a very driven person with big goals.

You know that you have work to do if you want to eventually earn a starting spot on the team. Not only do you have upper-classmen ahead of you, but nobody really knows you. Your coaches and teammates have no idea what your work ethic is like or how you will perform on and off the field or court. You will need to consistently prove to them that you are an asset to the team. Even if you were highly recruited in high school, you haven't proven anything at this level yet.

Now, let's assume you are of the mindset that you are going to do whatever it takes to earn your spot. You are more motivated than at any other time in your athletic career, and you are ready to go to work! There's just one problem: Your roommates aren't as driven as you are. You have two roommates, and they are on completely different ends of the motivation spectrum. One roommate is the most highly recruited freshman in program history with a full-ride scholarship and all the natural ability in the world. The other is an average athlete whose well-to-do parents knew someone who pulled some strings to open a place on the team, and they are also footing all the bills.

It's your first night on campus, and fall training starts the next day. Your roommates are excited to meet new people and want to go partying. They want to put down the top on the convertible, get some beer, and cruise around town before hitting up house parties. What do you do? The star recruit is asking you to hang out! It's only one night, so what's the big deal? Are you really going to blow off everyone and just chill in your dorm room by yourself? You decide to tag along, but you're only going to have a couple drinks and not get too crazy because you have practice tomorrow.

Things don't quite go as planned. You return to your dorm at 4 a.m. after partying all night. Your roommate backed the car into another one in the parking lot, and you lost your cell phone. You "bonded" with your teammates, though, and the star recruit thinks you're pretty cool! The three of you decide to get a couple hours of sleep before heading to morning conditioning, but you oversleep your alarm and show up to conditioning 30 minutes late.

Your coaches want the team to learn a lesson, so they make examples out of you. They make you run laps for the duration of practice and clean up all the gear afterward. Then it gets worse: You throw up, and there's no hiding the fact that you're hungover.

You learned your lesson, but your roommates did not. Two months in, they are partying almost every night and going through the motions during class. They give a decent effort at practice and in the weight room, but people are noticing something isn't right. On the other hand, you go out from time to time, but you don't drink. You are doing everything you can in the gym and in class to prove yourself, but you keep getting lumped in with them. It seems as though your reputation was solidified the first day, and you're not sure what to do moving forward. Something has to change. How long can you be around them before you begin to drink and head down the same path they are on?

Ultimately, you decide to request a transfer out of your dorm. You explain the situation, and your request is granted. The downside is your roommates no longer talk to you and the star recruit has sworn to make your life miserable for making them look bad. However, everything falls into place when you meet your new roommates. Both of them are walk-ons who got into school more on the strength of their GPAs and ACT scores than their athletic ability. They both have a goal of starting by their junior year.

Your whole life turns around. It takes a while, but the three of you become the best of friends. You make a pact to hold each other accountable and even hang a progress chart in your room. Every morning you are up early to go running. Then, you eat breakfast together before class. In the weight room you can't be stopped. Nobody works harder than you three. You bring an energy and drive to succeed that your coaches say they've never seen. Practices are difficult, but you're improving as a player, and the three of you are always encouraging your teammates. You're the first ones in and the last ones out of practice each day. You prioritize school and finish your first year with 4.0 GPAs. You don't see playing time during your freshman year, but a foundation has been laid, and everyone knows it. Your time will come.

To be successful, you must surround yourself with like-minded people. At some point, sustaining a negative relationship cannot be strictly about how much you care for that person or how far back your friendship goes. If someone is constantly dragging you in a negative direction, you have to let go. You cannot continually put yourself in situations that are detrimental to your goals and still expect to reach your goals. Of course, friendship is important, and you can absolutely try to positively influence the people around you. However, you have very limited control over other people, and every bit of energy you spend attempting to change others is energy not spent on yourself and your goals.

How do you know when to cut ties and move on? The problem is that most people find the answer to this question much too late. Look for signs that a person, or a group of people, may not be the best influence on you. Ask about goals and aspirations. Talk about values. Do theirs line up with yours? Let's say you have dreams of going to college and playing sports, and your "friends" smoke pot, get poor grades, and say college is overrated. Do you think spending time with them will help you achieve your goals? No. As a matter of fact, the more time you spend with them, the less likely you are to even get into college. Instead, seek out friends who are never late to school, get good grades, and enjoy playing sports. Look for people that also go above and beyond in everything they do. Spend your time with those who talk about their goals and are excited to pursue them with drive and determination. The positive energy of those people will propel you to be better, and you will do the same for them. This leads to a productive culture.

In sports, in a classroom, at work, or even at home, culture matters. Culture is the general vibe you get from being part of a team at any level. It cannot be faked, but it can be changed. You are as much a team with your family as you are with your peers in the sports you play. You are on a team with your teachers and fellow students, and you are on a team with your coworkers.

The combined attitudes of individuals determine the culture of a team. Attitude can be defined in a number of different ways, but I define it as "A set of core values acted upon daily."

Our gym's core values are:

1. Be positive.
2. Control your effort.
3. Care about others.

One poor attitude among our gym staff of 10 people will not ruin the culture that has been developed over a decade. However, that doesn't mean it won't go unnoticed. I work very carefully to eliminate any negativity as soon as it pops up. If I let a person with a bad attitude influence other employees, it will become a problem. Three or four selfish people complaining, showing up late to work, and putting forth a half-hearted effort will have a detrimental effect on our gym culture. Not only will other employees see this, but our members will as well. Before long, people will stop showing up to the gym because the vibe isn't positive and fun.

The culture of a team stems from the attitudes of the people at the top and trickles down. Teachers are responsible for the culture of their classrooms. Parents are responsible for the culture in their families. Coaches are responsible for the culture of their teams. A business owner is responsible for employee culture. This goes one step further in a service-based business because employees are responsible for the culture within the customer base.

A team is a well-oiled machine when everyone is on the same page, with a good attitude, on a daily basis. People will have bad days, but complete buy-in on a solid set of core values will ensure the culture stays intact through difficult times. Take a deeper dive into our core values to understand exactly why they define our culture and have led to the success of our gym.

- A positive attitude means you are not complaining. You bring energy and brightness to everything you do. You make life more fun for those around you. Your attitude is infectious, and people enjoy spending time with you.
- Controlling your effort means you worry about yourself. You give 100% to everything you do. You show up early. You stay late. You do things without being asked. You do not let someone else's lack of effort bother you. If you want something, you go work for it. You understand that you are the only person responsible for your success.
- Caring about others means you are not selfish. You are able to be goal driven while putting others first. You build

relationships with people because their well-being matters to you. You are genuine in your actions and want to have a positive impact on the lives of others.

It is through these core values that our culture thrives.

The simplest way to ensure consistent self-growth is to not be the smartest person in the room. Always surround yourself with people better than you. This means putting your ego aside and getting comfortable with being uncomfortable, because you are going to be challenged. Success is contagious. Find people who have what you want and learn from them. Take every opportunity you get to grow and develop yourself. But remember that it is easy to get so caught up in the end goal that you miss the magic of the journey. Learn to fall in love with the process.

Imagine a group of elite-level greyhounds chasing a mechanical rabbit around a track. It is because of that rabbit that they reach world class speeds. Slow down the rabbit, and the dogs will slow as well. Their ultimate goal is to catch the rabbit. It's not the process of trying to catch the rabbit that pushes them. They aren't in love with the training. They know nothing of their nutrition and training regimen. It's the thrill of the chase and the anticipation of catching the rabbit that keep the dogs going. They are so goal-oriented that if they caught the rabbit, they would immediately stop running. Unlike greyhounds, we have the ability to think on a deeper level. We can grow to the point where the process is more important than the goal itself.

Some goals you will reach, and some you won't. If you accomplish every goal you set, then you are not setting the bar high enough in the first place. Make your goal like that rabbit. If you catch it, make it faster the next time. Keep raising the bar. It's not the finish line that keeps you going, but rather the thrill of the chase. If you do make it to the top, be aware that you will have become the rabbit and people will be chasing you. Never stop pushing yourself to be better. Never allow yourself to be caught.

You are responsible for your success. You choose who you spend time with. Every minute wasted with unproductive, negative, lazy people is a minute in which you are not working towards your goals. Remove those people from your life. The company you keep should be driven and motivated, like you. They should lift you up and make you a better person. Ultimately, your character reflects the character of the few people you spend the most time with.

## FINAL THOUGHTS

Choose your friends wisely. Your character reflects the character of the few people you spend the most time with. Surround yourself with people who are better than you; this is how you grow.

## REFLECTION

1. Look back at your reflection for Chapter 1. Do the people you surround yourself with align with your values?
2. What is an example of a negative culture you have been a part of?
3. What is an example of a positive culture you have been a part of?

CHAPTER 3

# ACT ELITE

Certain people stand out in a crowd. They command attention seemingly effortlessly. Others are drawn to them and long for that sort of star power. What makes these people stand out from everyone else? How do you become one of those people? Look beyond fame and good looks. The real answer is a combination of things that can be taught and practiced. It's the way you carry yourself. It's your body language. It's the language you use. It's the sincerity with which you communicate. It's confidence in the person you are and the way you treat people. It's not talent or genetic potential. Anyone can learn these behaviors, but they must be consistently practiced to be effective.

Most importantly, always act like someone is watching. This single rule could eliminate 90% of the mistakes people make. As a kid, imagine your parents or teachers are watching your every move. As a player on a team, imagine your coach is by your side in class, in the gym, and at home. As a married person, imagine your spouse is always right there with you. Not only do they see your actions, but they also hear everything you say. Do you think you would act differently or choose your words more wisely? How do you drive when a police officer is behind you? Would you say to someone's face the things you post on social media or send in a text? If you are comfortable with your words and actions, then you will have nothing to hide. A person's true character shines brightest when no one is looking.

## Walk tall.

Throw your shoulders back and stand with confidence. Be proud of the things you have accomplished and the path you are on. Your hard work and dedication are leading to your success. Do not slouch or shy away from attention. If people gravitate to you, they are doing it for a reason. Share your experiences with them, and let your positive energy radiate into those around you. At the same time, there is a fine line between confidence and arrogance. Crossing it will turn people away from you. Walk tall while remaining humble. Appreciate the opportunities that you were afforded, and remember that nobody does this alone.

## Look people in the eyes and shake hands.

A confident person, with nothing to hide, will look people in the eyes when talking to them. We teach our young athletes how to communicate with prospective coaches and authority figures. A quality introduction starts with a firm handshake. As you shake hands, meet the eyes of the person you are talking to. Additionally, sound excited about meeting that person! First impressions can make or break your opportunity. You may not always get weeks, months, or years to show someone the kind of person you are, so you need to make a lasting impact in just a few moments. Let's analyze a few scenarios.

- **Interviewing for a job.** You get one shot to stand out from everyone else applying for the same job. Of course, your résumé and the way you answer questions will matter. However, starting off on the right foot makes a big differ-ence. You need to grab the attention of the person inter-viewing you and give him/her a reason to be excited about you as a potential employee. As a business owner, I can assure you that a person who shakes my hand and looks me in the eyes when applying for a job will make an immediate impact. That person will have my full attention, and I will be actively engaged in the conversation. I am going to assume the way a person introduces themselves to me is also the way they will interact with clients and customers at my gym.

- **Meeting the parents of the person you are dating.** This means that you will be judged and picked apart on every level. Parents simply want the very best for their children, and that includes the people they choose to date. Perhaps in this situation more than any other, a negative first impression will linger the longest. I am a father to two beautiful girls. Someday I will have boys wanting to date my daughters. At that time, young men will be asking me to trust them with the well-being of two of the most important people in my life. Assuming this is in high school, that means I am turning over 16 years of my care and love to someone I just met. Those boys better make a very good impression. I expect them to look me in the eyes, shake my hand, and be able to have a genuine conversation with me. As they leave, I expect to hear "thank you" and "it was nice to meet you." Finally, if they don't hold the door for my girls, they will never walk back through mine.
- **Making a campus visit to your top-choice college.** This is the school you want to attend more than any other. Perhaps you are not only choosing this school for the academics, but you are also hoping for an athletic scholarship. Even if you are being recruited, realize that dozens of other kids are, too. A coach will certainly have watched film of your games and looked at your grades. They have done their homework prior to inviting you for a visit. Assuming all other things are equal, you will need to do something to "wow" the coach. Kick things off with a greeting that encompasses a bold look in the eyes, a strong handshake, and an excited "It's nice to meet you, Coach!" Your positive impression will be made. That sort of energy and attitude is exactly what any college coach would want in a player. A story I heard some time ago on ESPN Radio about the NBA draft was so eye-opening that it is one I regularly share with our athletes. A team's general manager was explaining his team's draft process and how they evaluate players.

The unique thing about this team was that they had a scout in place to evaluate the body language of players. The scout would watch film of players every time they came out of a game. He was watching to see if the players threw towels, punched chairs, and ignored coaches, or if they were generally positive, high-fived teammates, and cheered from the sidelines. Did they stay actively engaged while on the bench, or did they seem to be checked out? The GM said that this evaluation process was the most important of the entire draft for his team. That story is one of the coolest ones I have ever heard about the evaluation of players. You can bet an enthusiastic handshake, with eye contact, matters to that team.

- **Working as a salesperson.** You could be selling cars, boats, stocks, insurance, fertilizer for crops, or services of any sort. The Number One rule in sales is to make a friend. Simply put, people do business with people they like and trust. Looking someone in the eyes shows that you are confident and believe in the product or service you are selling. Shaking someone's hand shows respect and that you are excited to do business with them. A salesperson who struggles with eye contact and neglects to shake the hand of a potential customer might as well be holding a giant red flag. It is difficult to earn trust and likability in a matter of minutes, so be sure to start with a reassuring introduction.
- **Meeting new people.** Let's suppose you're meeting a new group or coworkers at a new job. In this case, you are going to be spending time with these people for the foreseeable future. Keeping quiet and shying away from others will not give the impression you want. Imagine walking into a workplace on your first day of employment. You have one of two options. The first is to go about your business and do your own thing. You have no need to go out of your way to make new friends or seek out coworkers to strike up conversation. After all, this is a job and nothing more. The other option is to smile, introduce yourself to people, shake their hands, and leave a positive first impression.

The latter will make your job more fun moving forward. People will be excited about coming to work and seeing you. Without even knowing it, you will have laid the foundation for your growth within the company as well. If you are going to spend 40-plus hours a week with people, why would you not make the most of that time?

Each scenario presents a situation in which a positive first impression will allow you to make the most of an opportunity. To be elite is to take full advantage of every opportunity you are given. It starts with a handshake.

## *Speak up.*

If you have something to say, say it with authority and purpose. The same words spoken in distinctly different ways will have distinctly different effects. A firm handshake and looking someone in the eyes will get a person's attention. Likewise, a well-spoken idea will provoke thought and engagement in return. For example:

You are up for a promotion at work. Your boss has given you and two other employees the opportunity to compete for the new position. The rules are simple. Whoever comes up with the best idea for the company to generate more revenue will earn the promotion.

You do your research and come up with an idea that is guaranteed to generate $100,000 in additional income the first year. Those numbers should increase at no less than 25% per year over the course of the next five years. This is actually something you have been working on since you were hired, so the timing couldn't be more perfect. The numbers support your idea, but it does mean an initial investment of $15,000 from the company.

Coworker John's plan will allow for $20,000 to $30,000 of revenue the first year, and projections show it tops out at $40,000. There is no initial investment from the company. John has been loud and boisterous, telling anyone who will listen about his new idea. He is sure he will win the promotion.

Coworker Sally develops a plan that shows a $90,000

additional revenue stream for the first year, and it calls for a $50,000 initial investment from the company. She has no data to back up her outlandish projections, but she claims her plan could generate as much as $250,000 per year.

From the outside looking in, your idea is the clear-cut winner. The biggest challenge is going to be your ability to present it to the management team. John's dad has been with the company for 20 years and is well-liked by everyone. That is why John is so confident in winning the promotion. Sally is a natural talker. She was a waitress in college, and she was the leading salesperson at the biggest car dealership in a three-state sales region for three years. Her ability to talk to people is intimidating. You are more reserved. You work hard, but aren't really into the social scene and have never held a sales job of any sort. Numbers are your thing, and you love your job. Your quiet demeanor is often mistaken for a lack of interest.

The three of you present your ideas to the management team at the next meeting. You go first. You stumble over your words and are clearly very nervous. You rehearsed your presentation a hundred times, but you forget two of your main talking points. Additionally, you get so flustered you cut the presentation short and don't even finish. John goes next. He drills home the fact that his idea costs nothing up front and that he is the safe bet. He seems to be selling himself more than his plan. Sally rocks it. Even though you know her far-fetched projections have no foundation, she almost convinces even you her plan will work. Her charisma and charm put her over the top, and ultimately, she wins the promotion. Three years later, nothing she promised has panned out, and management knows they made the wrong decision.

In that one presentation, you failed. You had an opportunity, and you let it slip away. Your lack of confidence and inability to speak to a group outweighed your knowledge. This actually happens frequently. More often than not, the most engaging, outwardly confident person in the room will be heard first. However, at some point, confidence with no roots will fail. If you are unsure about what you are saying, or if you don't have presentation skills, it will show when you talk. Knowledge is key. Knowledge gives you the ability to present your thoughts with confidence. You must be able to then speak in an effective manner. From there, piece everything together. Look people in the eyes, speak up, and be eloquent in doing so.

## *The way you speak matters.*

The manner in which you speak carries as much weight as the words themselves. Being polite and using an appropriate tone can be the difference between getting what you want and not. A motivational speaker, a drill sergeant, a patron at a restaurant, and a spouse all speak in different tones. The tone you carry is determined by both the person to whom you are speaking and the situation at hand.

A motivational speaker may use a variety of tones when delivering a speech to a group. If the end goal is to create excitement, a soft, mellow, laid-back tone will simply not do the job. A louder, emphatic, energetic tone will grab the attention of the audience and keep them engaged. Imagine the captain of a football team delivering a pregame speech just before taking the field. What kind of tone will he use to get his teammates fired up?

A drill sergeant certainly uses loud tones when speaking to recruits. For the duration of most drills, there really is no such thing as a caring or kind tone. This is a very unique situation meant to create the most mentally strong soldiers.

You can be sure that at some point you will be frustrated when dining out. A cook will mess up your order. You will get stuck with a new waiter who forgets things. There will be screaming kids in the booth next to you. Your service will be slower than you like. How you handle those situations will determine your experience. For the most part, nobody is intentionally trying to mess up your meal out. Taking a deep breath and being patient will make things better for everyone involved.

Suppose you are out to eat with a few friends at the end of a long week at work. Your food arrives in a timely way, but your steak is undercooked and you have the wrong side. You could handle the situation in a number of ways, but we are going to look at two responses.

- **Response A:** You say to the waiter in an angry and sarcastic tone, "Take this back! This isn't what I ordered. Are you new here? Do you have trouble following instructions? How hard can it be?"
- **Response B:** You smile and calmly say to the waiter, "Hey, I know you're busy, but my order isn't quite right. Would it be possible to have my steak cooked a little longer? Also, I ordered green beans and not mashed potatoes. Could I please get a side of green beans?"

Response B will generate a much more favorable response from your waiter. Additionally, your mood moving forward will be more positive and lead to the evening turning out well in the end. You can't change what has already happened. However, your words and the way in which you say them will have a direct effect on the remainder of the night.

The way you speak to your spouse or significant other is the one which should get the most consideration from you. You are planning to spend the majority of your life with that person, so your words carry more weight than those spoken to a stranger. Of course, there will be ups and downs in any relationship. Couples disagree with each other often. It is likely that some disagreements will escalate farther than they should. Slowing down, taking a deep breath, and thinking before you speak will help you avoid saying things in a hurtful manner. Always consider where the other person is coming from. Do your very best to see the situation from a point of view other than your own. Stay calm and do not raise your voice. Doing these things will allow for healthy conversations without guardedness. Love for someone includes respect for that person. Few things show respect more than the words and tone you use when speaking to someone.

Consider your audience when speaking. Every person responds uniquely to various tones and words. Your ability to understand and relate to your audience is key to getting your point across.

### Be the kind of person you would want your child to marry.

This really hits home if you have kids, but you can certainly understand the concept even if you have no children. As a father of two daughters, it is hard for me to imagine them being anything other than Daddy's little girls. Looking back on my wedding day from the perspective of a father of girls, I realize how much trust my in-laws put in me to take care of their daughter. The men who marry my daughters will be expected to show them the same love, care, loyalty, and patience that I do. I want my girls to know how they should be treated. I want them to look for a man who has the same qualities I have. If you are unsure if you want your children to marry someone like yourself, it's time to make some changes in your life.

### Hold the door for others.

The simple act of holding the door for another person shows kindness, selflessness, and respect. It takes mere seconds, and it could change someone's day in a way you couldn't expect. You never know what another person is going through, and in that moment you can make a positive impact. Don't just hold the door. Smile. Say hello, and speak sincerely.

Men, always hold the door for the woman in your life. Women, for all the reasons previously mentioned, let a man hold the door for you.

### Be with someone who makes you a better person.

I've seen the way good relationships can positively impact lives, and I've also seen how devastating bad ones can be. I am very close with my mom. She has done more for me and provided me with more opportunities than anyone else in my life. She is an incredible woman, and I am blessed to have her for a mother. My biological father was an alcoholic. He was mentally and physically abusive to my mom. He walked out when I was two years old and never paid child support. My mom did remarry, but that relationship also ended in divorce. My stepdad is a good man, but simply not the kind to go above and beyond to lift my mom up or better their relationship. The one thing I wish my mom had is a quality man to inspire her and do for her what she has done for so many people.

I encourage you to consider your own relationship. Does your boyfriend, girlfriend, husband, or wife bring out the best in you? Is that person consistently building you up or tearing you down? Is your significant other the kind of person you would want your child to marry?

In a positive relationship, both people should be good individuals, and as a team they should be even better. In sports, teammates are there for each other. When someone is having a rough game, the team is there to pick up the slack. There will be losses along the way, but a strong team stays together. The best teams are consistently improving. Players end up knowing each other's subtleties and thoughts. With enough time, they don't have to ask; they just "know." Other teams look at them and want what they have. Without meaning to do so, they become the gold standard. A healthy relationship should mirror those teams.

Being part of a team goes well beyond practices and games. The teams with the best chemistry choose to hang out together off the field or court in their spare time. In a relationship, particularly a marriage, people should want to spend time together outside of the home. You can't fake camaraderie. You either have it or you don't, and, if you don't consistently work on it, you will lose it.

I've been part of teams with the "it" factor. It is so cool to be a family of brothers all banded together for a common goal. The game-time intensity is incredible, and there's a certain swag that makes it so much fun to play together. The relationships off the field were a big part of what made those teams click. Whether driving to and from games, eating with the guys, or just chilling together, we made memories to last a lifetime. Even though I haven't seen some of those guys in years, we could pick up right where we left off. That kind of bond takes teams to a new level.

The kind of bond that gives teams the "it" factor should be present in a relationship as well. In a marriage, couples who are always looking to get out of the house and hang with friends will drift apart. Friendships with like-minded people are positive, but no friendship is more important than the relationship with your spouse. Couples need to spend time together doing things that friends do together. Your best friend should be the person you married. Your spouse is the person you will spend the rest of your life with, so you need to put more time and effort into that relationship than any other. You know you have something special when you pick up the phone simply to chat, you are excited to get home, and the two of you would choose spending time together instead of choosing to do anything else.

No individual is bigger than the team, and teammates who genuinely care about each other will be the most successful. The same goes in your relationship. Your teammates, boyfriend, girlfriend, husband, or wife should all make you better. In turn, you should have the same impact on them.

### Randomly do nice things for others without looking for recognition.

One way you can positively affect the lives of others is to do nice things for them. These acts of kindness can be planned or spontaneous. They can be grand in gesture or very simple. What you do pales in comparison to the thought behind your actions.

## FINAL THOUGHTS

Act as though your loved ones are always watching. Do things that would make them proud. Stand out in a crowd. Walk with confidence and, when you shake someone's hand, look them in the eyes. Hold the door for others, and do the little things that matter, especially when nobody is looking.

## REFLECTION

1. Can you think of someone who stands out in a crowd? Why?
2. The last time you met someone new, how did you greet them?
3. Have you ever felt intimidated or unsure when speaking?
4. Does your tone change depending on who you speak with?
5. What relationship or team have you been a part of that had great chemistry?

CHAPTER 4

# THINK, THEN REACT

There is an old rule of thumb when it comes to negotiating and sales: "Whoever speaks first loses." Most people are uncomfortable with silence and tend to back down when an opposing party doesn't say anything. In a sales example, when you receive an offer for less than you want, be silent for as long as possible. Wait and see what happens. Often, the party presenting the offer will begin to question themselves. They may even present a better one without you having to say a word.

Listen first. Think second. Speak third. When you talk, you cannot actively think about what someone has just said to you. Instead, you are thinking only about the words coming out of your mouth. If you're too quick to speak, your words are probably emotionally driven and come out with little thought.

Listening first shows respect to the person whom you are engaging in conversation. Additionally, giving the other person the opportunity to speak in full will allow you to process what is said in its entirety. Be sure to take in everything that is said, and do not get stuck on a few words. It is easy to get hung up on one thing and tune a person out as you formulate a response in your head. Actively listen first, and then take a few moments to generate a well-thought-out response. This applies to conversations in person, via email, or through text messages.

Do not engage in debates of any kind on social media platforms. This one rule will do more for you than you could ever imagine.

There are a handful of things you can do to ensure success in conversation. This does not mean you will win every argument or debate you engage in, and that isn't the point. It means you will give yourself the best chance at productive communication that leads to some sort of positive outcome.

### Be patient in conflict.

Being patient in a difficult conversation carries two meanings. Always first listen to someone as they speak and do not hurry to respond. Rushing to tell a person they are wrong will accomplish nothing. Instead, it will cause them to throw up walls, and productivity in that moment will be difficult. With that in mind, it is okay to table a conversation for another time. When you feel passionately about a topic, it is natural to want to solve the problem immediately. However, there are situations when temporarily halting a discussion is for the best. Allowing everyone to cool off, take a step back, and process things can lead to real productivity later. Maybe the conversation needs just an hour's break, or maybe it needs a few days. Do not, however, let things go unresolved for so long that feelings of animosity and resentment begin to build. Patience in immediate conversation and the willingness to take a break will produce positive results for everyone involved.

### Wear their shoes.

We've all heard the saying, "Put yourself in their shoes." As an adolescent, I brushed this off every time my parents said this to me. It wasn't until much later in life that I truly grasped the importance of those words. Looking at it backwards is the best way to understand what it means. How many times have you said or thought, "If you only knew…" or "You wouldn't understand…"? Imagine you had the ability to let others experience exactly the emotions and sensations you feel in a situation. While there is no real way to do that, doing so would certainly make communication much easier. That's what putting yourself in someone else's shoes means.

Another great way to empathize with someone is to reflect on your past experiences. Even if you have never gone through exactly what they are, odds are you have experienced something similar at some point. Recalling how you felt during that time will allow you to better understand their perspective. Remember that you are in no hurry to speak. Take the time to view things from every angle before rushing to form an opinion.

### Educate yourself.

The idea of educating yourself correlates with your ability to not believe everything you see on social media, read on the internet, or see on the news. With so much information readily available at the touch of a button, there is no excuse for failing to educate yourself on any topic. However, you need to be very careful when selecting your sources. Be sure that you read reputable material and only listen to people with a solid résumé. Anyone, anywhere, can put something on the internet and make it look real. The increasing use of AI to create content can result in combinations of half-truths that can look legitimate. It is up to you to decipher what is fact and what is fiction, opinion, or outright falsification — and more often than not, those lines are blurred. Making things even more complicated is that for every article you read leaning one way, there will be another leaning the opposite way. You have a responsibility to do as much research as possible to form your own opinion. The worst thing you can do is speak about something of which you are underinformed. Ultimately, you are responsible for the words you say and type.

### Wait 24 hours when using social media.

Anything on social media that triggers a negative emotion within you should not be commented on for 24 hours. More than ever, people today are realizing that once something is on the internet, including social media, it never goes away. Things from a decade ago or more are coming back to bite athletes, coaches, movie stars, and other famous people. While you may never have thousands of people viewing what you post on social media, rest assured that someone of importance will see it. Simply put, if something gets you fired up, leave it alone. At the very least, wait 24 hours to respond with less emotion attached.

## *You are not always right.*

Often, we get so hung up on winning an argument that we fail to accomplish what we set out to do in the first place. It is better to learn than to be right. Focusing on a common goal, in a spirit of cooperation and humility, leads to resolution.

More important than what you are trying to accomplish is why you are doing it. For example, deciding where to go on family vacation isn't about the destination as much as it is about spending time together. Arguments are going to happen; it is extremely rare for people to always see eye to eye. Shifting your focus from the "what" to the "why" will allow for more productive discussions. Remember, the best solution to a problem with two sides usually falls somewhere in the middle.

Thinking first and reacting later helps to remove emotion from decision-making. The longer you wait to respond to something, the less emotion will be involved. Time gives you the opportunity to examine a situation from all angles and educate yourself before speaking and/or making a decision.

Additionally, behaviors that feel good in the moment are often those you will regret later. Alcohol abuse leads to drunk driving and a range of health problems. The nicotine from cigarettes gives you a high, but smoking can lead to lung cancer. Cheating on your spouse often leads to divorce. A diet consisting of fried, processed, and sugary foods may taste good, but it leads to heart disease and obesity. A social media post could cost you your friends, job, or spot on a team. Buying a new pair of shoes for $100 would look cool, but that same $100 could mean thousands of dollars in your retirement. Take the time to think about the big picture and what you are trying to accomplish. Focus on the "why" more than the "what." Ask yourself what you want the long-term outcome to be. Are your decisions going to lead to your success down the road?

## FINAL THOUGHTS

It is impossible to think clearly when upset. Wait 24 hours before you post anything on social media. Once it's out there, you can't take it back. Avoid impulse decisions and things that feel good in the moment. Keep your goals in mind, and make decisions based on what will help you reach them. Always listen, then think, and then react. Doing so in this order matters.

## REFLECTION

1. When is a time you responded too quickly out of emotion?
2. Name a situation in which you wished someone could walk in your shoes?
3. How can educating yourself lead to more productive discussion?

CHAPTER 5

# CONTROL YOUR EFFORT

Our gym's core values set the tone for everything we do.

1. Be positive.
2. Control your effort.
3. Care about others.

These core values are discussed with coaching staff and members alike. They are displayed prominently in the gym for everyone to see. We believe that if every person fully embraces them, our gym will have the ability to change lives for the better. In this chapter, we are going to delve into what it means to control your effort.

The first thing that you must buy into is that you are the only person who has the ability to change your life, for better or worse. Stop pointing fingers and putting blame elsewhere. Ultimately, you are responsible for everything you have or don't have. If you want to change your status quo, then go to work and do something about it!

There are two scenarios I see every day that directly relate to a person's ability to control their effort. The first is young athletes training to improve for sports. The second is people looking to be healthier through exercise and proper nutrition. Everyone tells me they want "it" badly. Most go so far as to say they will do whatever it takes to be successful. All too often, when people find out exactly what it really takes to reach their goals, they aren't willing to complete the process.

Over the years I have changed my outlook and my approach to coaching. Early on, if someone didn't want to put in the effort, I didn't want to waste my time with them. I knew what they needed to do, and if they weren't willing to do it, then I moved on. My mindset is completely different today. I eventually figured out that most people simply don't know what they're getting into. They have good intentions, but they genuinely have no way of knowing. Most people have never experienced the kind of discipline, effort, and energy it takes to turn their lives around. So, it is my job to pour every ounce of my effort into people to make sure that they are successful. Today, I choose to take the approach that if someone fails on my watch, then it is my fault. I could've done something different. If I would've found a better way to connect with them, maybe they would've reached their goals. Intellectually I know I can't help everyone, but with this mindset I have a much better shot at doing so.

We have a variety of programs for youth that range from well-rounded fitness to in-depth athletic prep training. We hang in our gym the high school jersey of each athlete who goes on to play college sports. Our annual Athlete Development Camp plays host to more than 80 youth each summer. Over the years, we have had more than 1,000 kids participate in our programs in some manner. At least half of them expressed a desire to play college sports.

When a kid says they want to play college sports, I sit down with them and explain what it is going to take to do so. Nearly every one of them walks out of my office, fired up, ready to give 100% effort. More often than not, the next day at the gym, I see them on their phones wasting time. In that moment, I know that I'm going to have a lot of work to do to change their habits.

I'll never forget a conversation I had with one young man. He came in to work out one afternoon for the first time in months. He was heavily involved in high school athletics and a very good athlete. He told me that his starting spot on the football team was in jeopardy. The coaches were thinking about moving one of his buddies into his role, which he seemingly had locked up. He was frustrated and started telling me how dumb it was and that everything was about "politics." In his head, he didn't do anything to lose his spot. I let him vent for a while about the situation. He went on to tell me it wasn't fair and that he was definitely the better athlete. I listened and then told him that I hadn't seen him in the gym for a while. I went on to ask what he had been up to and if he had been working out somewhere else. His response solidified what I already knew. He said that he hadn't been doing much since he heard he might lose his spot and just wasn't feeling up to working out. That was my cue for a fantastic teaching moment.

Controlling my urge to raise my voice, I explained to him why his thinking was backwards. First, I can't think of too many coaches who wouldn't play the players who were the best at their position and also deserved to play. I guaranteed him that if I were his coach making that decision, his lack of effort would've cost him his spot regardless of his talent. All he needed to do was flip his thinking to be successful. When he found out that his spot was on the line, he should've decided to do everything he possibly could to earn the position. Instead of skipping the gym for a few months, he should've put in two-a-days. He should've asked his coach what he needed to do to improve and help the team. He should've poured every ounce of his energy into making himself a better player and teammate. He should've come to me for help, and we would've started by making a list:

1. Lift at 5:30 a.m.
2. Watch film three times a week.
3. Come to CrossFit classes six times a week.
4. Train with me on sport-specific skills twice a week.
5. Follow a nutrition plan.
6. Go to bed every night by 9:30 p.m.

If he'd spent the preceding three months executing the things on this list, his life would've looked a lot different. Whether he actually earned the starting spot or not is second-ary to the positive habits that would've developed from the process. As an athlete and a person, he would've come away better.

But he hadn't even given himself a chance. Instead, he gave up and took himself out of the picture. Maybe his coach was looking for him to step up and be a leader. Maybe his coach was using this as a teaching moment for him. It wasn't too late, but he wasted a lot of time and needed to make changes immediately.

In fact, he did just that. He decided to do everything he could to earn that starting position. He got back to work, and I saw a renewed sense of energy in him. How did things turn out? A few months later, he ended up getting the starting spot and played the entire season.

Learn to love the process. Embrace effort. The journey is more important than the destination. The person you will become is the "why." The goal is the "what." The "why" is always more important than the "what. "

We have built a very successful nutrition business over the last decade. We have helped hundreds of people lose thousands of pounds of body fat. However, for as many people as we have positively impacted, there are a large number whom we couldn't seem to help.

People seek help with the intention of changing their lives. They often tell us they will do whatever it takes and they know they need to change habits. They are eager to listen and 99% of the time they walk out of our initial consult fired up and ready to attack the world. Then, something happens. They figure out it's not easy. Changing bad habits you've spent 20 years developing doesn't happen overnight. If it took a person 20 years to gain 100 pounds, they won't lose it in a couple months (in a healthy way). No matter how much accountability and motivation coaches try to provide, they give up. Sometimes it takes weeks and other times it takes months, but they fall right back into the same unhealthy lifestyle they sought to change. Why? Was it something we didn't do, or a lack of support on our end? What led to their failure?

The answer is simple: It comes down to effort. At some point, you must look yourself in the mirror and hold yourself accountable. I can give a client every tool and resource they need to be successful. I can provide coaching, insight, education, motivation, and support. However, I can't cook every meal and spoon-feed them. I can't follow them around making sure they don't eat junk food or stray from their plan. In the end, effort dictates outcome.

Most people are looking for easy answers. They are convinced — and led to believe from clever marketing — that there's a way to lose fat that doesn't involve good, old-fashioned hard work and discipline. They don't want to hear that the way to stay lean and healthy is to eat whole foods and exercise. That's no different than a teenage kid looking for an easy way to get a full-ride scholarship to play college football. It won't happen because of cool-looking gear, $300 shoes, or special YouTube gurus. It comes down to effort and hard work. Hit the gym. Work out with purpose and intent. Eat healthy and practice your craft. Do those things better than everyone else, and you will have it made. When talent is equal, effort will prevail.

These rules pertaining to effort will take you farther than you ever could imagine.

## Rule 1: Never hit snooze.

We've all heard this, and most of us have heard it multiple times. If everyone says it, there must be something to it, right? There is. If you don't hit snooze, you will have extra time in the morning. You will not be rushed to get out the door. You won't be late to work or school. You will eat breakfast, make the bed, read, and do a few chores. You will notice a change in how you approach everything you do, and you may even start waking up without an alarm. Not hitting snooze is a strong foundation for you to build upon. People who don't hit snooze are just different. They approach life with vigor and tenacity. They don't wait for opportunities to come to them; they seek them out!

## Rule 2: Talk less and do more.

The people around you are going to notice the things you do more than the things you say. Open-ended promises leave you and those around you unfulfilled. Imagine a parent who promises to spend time with their kids but never does. Imagine a kid who promises to clean their bedroom but always finds an excuse not to. Imagine someone who is late to everything but who always says they will be early next time. Think about the cocky athlete who is always running their mouth. They aren't afraid to tell the world how great they are. They get away with it until the game-time performances begin to slip.

It's easy to talk when things are going your way. There is a fine line between swag and arrogance. Err on the side of humility, and always be willing to do the work. You will be remembered for the things you do, not what you say you will do.

### Rule 3: Always do more than the minimum.

Doing what you are told, asked, and/or expected to do is acceptable. However, doing the minimum work requirement won't get you where you want to go. Taking shortcuts, looking for an "easy button," and just getting by is what the average person does. You want to be elite. People who are the very best at anything always do more than they have to. If your teacher tells you to read 20 pages in a book, read them twice. If your coach tells you to shoot 50 free throws, shoot 100. If your boss tells you a project is due Friday, get it done by Thursday. Show up early. Stay late. Overprepare. People will notice, and opportunities will begin to present themselves to you.

### Rule 4: Don't fear failure.

To fail in the act of hard work is acceptable; to fail because of the absence of effort is not. Additionally, the greater the risk, the greater the reward. Aim for the stars, set the bar high, and dream big! If you give 100% of yourself to anything, but come up short, you will still walk away better than you started. You will have gained experience, knowledge, and appreciation for the process. If you are afraid to put yourself out there, you will always wonder what could have been. Don't focus on what could go wrong. Set your sights on all the good that could come from your efforts. If you fail, get up and try again. You will fail again, but rest assured that someday you will reap the rewards of your hard work.

## Rule 5: No excuses.

If you want something, be so good they can't say no. Life is going to seem unfair from time to time. You can make excuses, or you can go to work to turn the tide in your favor. Someone else will get the promotion you wanted. Someone else will take the starting spot on the basketball team. Some people are going to be more naturally gifted than you. How you choose to deal with those situations will ultimately determine your success.

Spud Webb played 12 years in the NBA, averaging nearly 10 points per game. Darren Sproles is a college football Hall of Famer who played 15 seasons in the NFL. He holds the record for the most all-purpose yards in a season at 2,696. Jose Altuve is an Major League Baseball player for the Houston Astros. In 12 seasons he has won a Most Valuable Player award, a World Series, three batting titles and a Gold Glove. What do all of these men have in common? They are all 5 feet, 6 inches tall. Without a doubt, they had to go above and beyond to have those kinds of careers. The cards were seemingly stacked against them, but they came out on top. Where so many other people their height would've made excuses, they seized every opportunity to get better. They eliminated weaknesses and improved upon their strengths. Next time things don't go your way, use it as fuel for your fire. Think of it as a reason to get back to work and come away better than before.

## Rule 6: Someone else wants it as much as you do.

Always remember that as much as you want something, someone else wants it just as much. Odds are they are working at least as hard as you to get it, too. Don't let that happen! Dorian Yates won the Mr. Olympia six consecutive times in the 1990s. He changed the bodybuilding game forever as the first "mass monster." His nickname is The Shadow. He earned that name because he would seemingly appear out of nowhere to compete, only to disappear again. He didn't make public appearances. He didn't seek fame and glory when others did. He was singularly focused. He trained with unrivaled intensity, with just a few people, in an old gym in Birmingham, England. Multiple times, he was offered good money to live and train in the United States. However, he never accepted any of those offers. He reasoned that living in the United States would offer distractions that could lead to him not winning the Mr. Olympia. He made sure that nobody would outwork him, and that mindset is what made him one of the greatest bodybuilders of all time.

Seek to be that person. Never be outworked and, just when you think you have done enough, remember that someone out there wants it as much as you do, if not more. A lot of things are out of your control. The one thing that you can control is your effort.

## FINAL THOUGHTS

Give all your effort to anything you do. You cannot control the effort of others, and nobody can control yours. You are responsible for your success.

## REFLECTION

1. Is your effort where it needs to be?
2. When considering the six rules of effort, how many do you follow, and where is there room for improvement?
3. What situations make it challenging for you to give maximum effort, and why?

CHAPTER 6

# ATTITUDE

Your attitude is directly correlated to how you approach life. "Be positive" is the first core value in our gym because it is the single most important thing for my business to be successful. Conversely, nothing has the ability to ruin my business more than negativity. I am asked all the time how I'm so happy all the time. My response is always, "I love what I do. Plus, if I wasn't chipper at 4 a.m., it would be pretty hard for me to expect people to do burpees."

Imagine this scenario: Your alarm goes off at 3:45 a.m. You get out of bed, still only half awake, throw some clothes on, and head to your CrossFit gym. When you walk in, you're not greeted with a "Good morning!" The music is turned off, and your coach is sitting on a bench looking at his phone. Class starts in fifteen minutes and people slowly trickle in. Nobody is really talking, and it's awkwardly quiet until the clock hits 4:30 a.m. At that point, your coach, clearly tired, explains the workout in a monotone that makes you want to go back to sleep. The class continues that way for the next 45 minutes, and everyone leaves. Not a single person hears "Goodbye" or "Have a great day."

How long would it be before you began to sleep in or look for another gym?

Instead, imagine showing up at that same gym at 4:15 a.m.

and being greeted with an enthusiastic, "Hey, John! How are you today, buddy?!" Then, your coach engages you in small talk — your soreness after yesterday's lunges, your son's teeball game — and welcomes each person the same way as they show up. There's a genuine smile on his face, and you wonder how many cups of coffee he already slammed that morning. When he explains the workout, he talks about how awesome it's going to be and reassures everyone that he will help each person throughout class. People joke aloud about how terrible burpees are, and he fires back with, "Yeah, but these are early morning burpees! They burn more calories and will get you those abs you've always wanted!" He wraps up the explanation, claps his hands, and says emphatically, "Let's do some fitness!" There is constant encouragement from your coach during the workout and each person gets a fist bump when finished. When you walk out the door, you hear, "Have a great day, John! See you tomorrow!"

Now, that's a coach who makes you want to get up at 3:45 a.m. to work out!

I approach every morning with purpose and know that I need to be at the very top of my game, no matter how early it is. Our first class is at 4:30 a.m. daily. I'm always out of bed before 3:30 a.m. I shower, drink a big glass of water, make coffee, and arrive at the gym by 4 a.m. Very rarely does anyone show up prior to 4:15 a.m., but I want to be sure the lights are on, the workout is up on the TV, the music is on, and I have time to organize my thoughts before anyone walks in. From there, I do everything I can to ensure that each person has the best hour of their day at my gym.

My enthusiastic approach to each day is as much for myself as it is for my gym members. A positive attitude leads to me being far more productive than I would be otherwise. Ninety-nine percent of the time, I am ready to attack the day and pour every ounce of my energy into all that I do. I love my job and everything that comes along with it. I get to change lives and hang out with friends all day! Generally speaking, I get five to six hours of sleep each night. I quickly learned that, even on average sleep, you can have a productive day. Your attitude hinges on mindset, your outlook on life, and your willingness to succeed.

Attitude is everything, and being positive in all that you do is a key for success. You can't fake it, either. People will see right through you. Find something you love to do, and be genuine in all your efforts. When you are in the right situation, being positive should come naturally. If you find that you're unhappy, change your situation. You can do something about it. You not only control your effort, but you also control your attitude. You can change any situation you're in.

## CHANGE YOUR ATTITUDE TO CHANGE A SITUATION.

Changing a negative situation that you are in may not be easy, but you do have the ability to do so. It will likely require some degree of pain or sadness, but it will be worth it. You will reach a point when it feels like a huge weight has been lifted. Focus on your long-term goals and put yourself first.

There are times in life when it's okay to be selfish. Getting out of a negative situation is one of those times. If something or someone is detrimental to your health or wellness, get rid of them. Health and wellness refer to your physical, emotional, and mental well-being. Changing your attitude is the key to making successful changes. Examine the following situations and how to change them:

### *A bad relationship (abusive or otherwise)*

I am not a relationship expert, but I believe some of my experiences and things I have learned watching others are valuable to relate. My biological father was an abusive alcoholic. My parents divorced when I was a toddler, and within a year, I never saw him again. I didn't meet my wife until I was 27, and my relationships up to that point provided much-needed lessons.

Statistics show that 50% of marriages end in divorce. While it's hard to say how many relationships a person has in their lifetime, it's clear that well more than 50% don't last. Odds are that at some point you will be in a relationship that isn't a healthy one. The key is getting out of it before it gets out of control. Clear examples of unhealthy relationships are those that are physically or emotionally abusive. We will focus on those.

The first step to getting out of a bad relationship is recognizing when you're in one. Jealousy, anger, and a lack of trust don't belong in a relationship. Physical and emotional abuse certainly don't belong, and the aforementioned things can lead to that abuse. Trust your closest friends. If they tell you to get out of a relationship, listen. Furthermore, if you are questioning whether or not you are in a good relationship, you probably know the answer. You can love and care about someone and still be in an unhealthy relationship with them.

Many things can lead to a relationship turning south. Both people could contribute to the problem, or it could be very one-sided. In either case, it needs to end. It's not about passing blame, who did what to whom, or who is right or wrong. It's about getting out of a negative situation and making space for a positive one.

Changing your attitude about your relationship will allow you to move on.

Smile (that can be difficult), and think about how happy you will be once you are removed from the situation you're in. Imagine how good you will feel once the weight of that relationship has been lifted. Don't dwell on all the negative things about your current situation. Instead, focus on all the incredible things that are in your future. Imagine how you will feel without the stress, worry, and hurt from your current relationship. A positive approach to what lies ahead will give you the strength you need to move on.

### Friends drinking, smoking, or doing drugs

The need for acceptance can be a driving force in any decision-making process. Pressure to fit in can make it easy to fall in line with the masses, especially when it seems that everyone is having fun. However, do not let the people around you define who you are. Be the person you want to be, and remember that your character reflects the character of the few people you spend the most time with.

Focusing on your goals gives you the ability to resist temptation and put things in perspective. Alcohol, tobacco, and drugs do not have any positive effects on your body or mind. No amount of them will enhance your performance in any capacity. Simply put, they are a detriment to everything an elite individual wants to accomplish. If you make a detailed plan of how you are going to reach your goals, it will certainly not include alcohol, tobacco, or drugs. Becoming elite means standing out from the crowd and doing the things that nobody else wants to do. It will be worth it. Your attitude should reflect where you want to go, not where you are currently.

## Getting bad grades

Approximately one of every 1,300 high school athletes and less than 2% of college athletes go on to play professionally. This means that education should be every athlete's top priority. Just as some athletes are genetically gifted, some people are naturally smarter than others. This means some people will simply have to put in more work to get equal results. That's life. You can choose to avoid weaknesses, or you can turn them into strengths. Imagine what would happen if you put the same effort into the things you dislike and are not good at as those you enjoy and come easy to you. Just as Mat Fraser was willing to put his pride aside and train with high-school kids, you, too, can turn weaknesses into strengths.

Struggling in school does not mean you should throw in the towel, but it does mean you have a choice to make. You can choose to make excuses, blame teachers, and get by with below-average grades. You can also choose to seek out tutors, spend extra time studying, and begin to prioritize school above other things. Take a "no excuses" approach to schoolwork like the most elite athletes take to their training. The benefits of studying more reach beyond the walls of the classroom. Positive habits, discipline, and attention to detail will be incredible additions to your arsenal of tools.

## Second string

Few things are more disheartening than genuinely doing everything you can to earn an opportunity and then not getting it. Working hard for something does not always guarantee you will get what you want. It does, however, guarantee you develop work ethic and quality habits that will last a lifetime.

Imagine putting in years of relentless work to earn a starting spot on your team. You did everything you possibly could to better yourself. You woke up at 5 a.m. every morning and hit the gym with purpose. You spent time with personal trainers, specialized coaches, and even worked with a coach to dial in your nutrition. Hands down, you have never been better. You are now the absolute best version of you. A week out from the start of the season, roster spots are released, and you are second string. You poured your heart and soul into what you love, and it wasn't enough.

It's natural to be disappointed. That means you care and you really wanted what you were working for. It's not okay to dwell on the situation. The elite respond with ferocity and a renewed sense of dedication. Adopt the mindset that you will be so good they can't say no. Get back to work and do the things that molded you into the best version of yourself. You may never earn that starting spot, but if you take this approach with everything you do, you will accomplish great things in life. More important than the outcome itself is the commitment to your craft and the positive habits that develop from your work.

## FINAL THOUGHTS

Be positive. Find the good in every situation, and never complain, because doing so will change nothing. Your attitude will either hinder or facilitate your goals. Realize that you cannot control certain things, but you can control how you react to everything. Learn to take responsibility for your actions and your success. Nobody else will care as much as you do.

## REFLECTION

1. When is a time when you changed your attitude to change a situation?
2. What is your typical response when something negative happens?

CHAPTER 7

# OWN YOUR ACTIONS

Learning to accept responsibility for your actions and words is something that takes most people a lifetime to master. When you can do this, your potential for growth is limitless. Own absolutely everything you do. It is impossible to execute a plan to remedy a situation if you are stuck passing blame. It does not matter who did what to whom. How you respond, and your actions moving forward, are key.

Sometimes it can be helpful to simplify things to the level of young children. If you have siblings or kids, you can relate to the following situation:

Seven-year-old Noah is playing cars nicely with his brother Cole, who's 5. Suddenly, screams roar out of both boys. "Give it back!" "Ouch, that hurt!" "Knock it off!" "No, it's mine!" "I had it first!" Dad runs over to the boys to get to the bottom of what is going on, hoping for a quick resolution. After separating the boys, he asks, "What happened?"

Noah exclaims loudly, "He took the car I was playing with."

Cole, without hesitation, fires back, "That's because he pushed my car off the track."

Noah then responds, "No, I didn't! Your car was in the way of mine!"

It continues like this for a few minutes until Dad sends the boys to their rooms until they can calm down.

Imagine how quickly the situation would have been defused if this is how the boys respond when Dad asks, "What happened?"

Noah exclaims loudly, "He took the car I was playing with!"

Cole takes a deep breath and says, "I did take your car. I'm sorry. I should have asked first."

Noah responds, "It's okay. I'm sorry I pushed your car off the track. I shouldn't have done that."

The problem was resolved easily in the second scenario because each of the boys took responsibility for his actions. Instead spending time alone in their rooms, they were able to go back to playing right away. With that being said, the odds of this happening are slim to none. The fear of getting in trouble and not wanting to accept responsibility outweighs the benefits that come with owning one's actions. It's instinctive for a person to do what they can to avoid discipline, and that's a hard habit to break. Doing so begins with not making excuses.

Some kids are raised with everything handed to them on a silver platter. Their parents open every door and provide all opportunities for them. Others are born into poverty. Their parents — or in many cases single parent — work multiple jobs with minimum pay to put food on the table. There is no money for new clothes or travel sports. Opportunities are never handed to these kids, and nothing comes easy. It may seem like the latter situation is worse, but each presents unique challenges. Furthermore, if a young person learns to make the most of what they have, they will undoubtedly go on to do great things.

It's hard to argue against the idea that those who are handed opportunities have it easier than others. However, that doesn't mean that they will grow up to be successful. Having opportunities has nothing to do with a person's work ethic. I see it every day in my line of work. There is an easy way to tell which kids will be successful. If all else is equal in giftedness and talent, the magic lies in those who make the most of every opportunity.

If they work as though they were handed nothing, they will go on to do incredible things. It's not the opportunities you are presented with that make you elite. It's what you do with those opportunities that makes you elite.

On the other hand, if you aren't naturally gifted with wealthy parents, that doesn't mean you can't do everything you dream of. You have the choice to make excuses or go to work. Remember, complaining will not change the situation you are in, but your effort can change it. Nobody is going to do it for you. It doesn't take $200 shoes to shoot 100 free throws every day. It doesn't take a $300 glove to throw a baseball with a friend. You don't need a gym membership to run sprints and do push-ups, lunges, and sit-ups. You can choose to get a job when your buddies choose to spend their time otherwise. You do not have to be a product of your environment. You can write your own story and be as successful as you want to be!

Today, owning your actions and words carries a different meaning than 20 years ago. The advent of social media changed our world and the way in which we communicate. Additionally, when something is posted on social media, it is there forever. No longer can a person claim their words were taken out of context or deny saying something in the first place. Always take time to think before you post something on social media. However, if you make a mistake, you need to own it.

## LEADERS OWN EVERYONE'S ACTIONS

Leaders are and should be held to different standards when it comes to their actions and those following them. While a person cannot control what someone else does, they can play a role in their course of action. Here are some examples.

### *Parents and kids*

As a father, I am doing everything I can to raise my girls in what I believe is the right way. I want them to grow up to be good humans who live by the things laid out in this book. I understand that there will be bumps in the road, but the kind of people my daughters will grow up to be is a reflection of how their mom and I raise them. If they struggle in any way, it is our job to guide them through those struggles. How they deal with adversity is a direct reflection of our influence on them. Nobody spends more time with our kids than we do; therefore, they are products of us.

My wife and I are responsible for:
- Who our kids hang out with
- If they drink alcohol underage
- How they treat others
- How they handle stress
- Their grades in school
- How they handle money
- How they take care of their belongings
- How they talk to others
- How they act in sports
- Their effort
- Their work ethic
- If they act grateful

Knowing that we are responsible for the actions of our children doesn't mean that we won't make mistakes. We absolutely will, and we will do our best to learn and grow from those mistakes. If one of our girls drinks alcohol at a friend's house at age 14, I will accept responsibility for that. I will also teach her to own her actions and accept responsibility for making that choice. If I choose to solely blame her, then I will not grow as a parent. Accepting responsibility is only part of the growth process. I will need to think about why she made that choice and what I could have done differently to make sure she didn't.

- Did she ever see her mom and me drink?
- Were we laughing and having fun while drinking?
- Did we talk to her about our experiences with alcohol?
- Did we tell her what to do if she is in that situation?
- Did we know all the other kids that were going to be at that house?
- Did we talk to the other parents and know their stance on alcohol?

*Becoming Elite*

While ultimately the decision to drink alcohol would be her choice, there must be some degree of accountability as parents. Nothing will be solved if we say that we did everything we could have done, pass the blame, and then punish our daughter. There needs to be repercussions for her actions, and we also would need to reflect on what we could have done differently. More change is likely to be accomplished if our daughter were to own her actions and my wife and I were to put in more effort moving forward.

There will almost always be blame to place on everyone involved in a situation. Even if one party is more directly responsible, reflecting on what you could have done differently yourself will lead to personal growth.

## Teacher and students

Teachers play a vital role in the development of children, and in some cases, they spend more time with a child than their parents do. For that reason, there is immense pressure on teachers to make sure their students develop into productive adults. It wouldn't be so difficult if every kid was eager to learn, respectful, followed directions, and put forth quality effort in the classroom. For every dedicated student, there is one who won't listen, puts forth little to no effort, is disrespectful, and doesn't want to be at school. A teacher's compassion, desire to mold young people, and the degree to which they care about their students is what makes them incredible. Where it would be easy to give up on the difficult kids, most teachers choose to put in extra effort to help them.

Having friendships with several teachers, I know the challenges they face day in and day out. We often share stories about their students whom I coach in the gym. Most of the time, our discussions are positive and filled with praise for the kids we have in common. However, there are also discussions about the difficult students they deal with and how hard it can be to handle them. Not a single time has a teacher ever said to me that they don't care about a student. It's always the opposite.

Many kids are filled with potential but choose to give no

effort to see that potential realized. Poor choices in friends, a bad family life at home, or a traumatizing incident can cause kids to give up on themselves. Those are the ones who need someone to believe in them and the lives that can be most impacted by a teacher. The more difficult the student, the more desire there is to help them. There seems to be an innate sense of personal responsibility for every life a teacher touches. They know that their actions will have a direct effect on how their students turn out. Good teachers own that responsibility and relish the opportunity to positively impact their students.

## Coach and players

Sports provide many valuable life lessons. Things like camaraderie, teamwork, how to handle adversity, and humility are often best taught on the field. Spearheading those lessons are the coaches. The difference between winning and losing can often be attributed to how tightly knit a team is and the members' commitment to one another. Coaches set the tone for their teams, and players look up to them like children to parents. Rarely will you see good coaches deflect blame to their players. The best ones accept responsibility for anything negative and place the spotlight on their players for all that is positive.

From recruiting to games, a coach controls everything about their team. A coach chooses the following:

- Their staff
- Delegation of duties to other coaches
- Whether or not to recruit talent above all else (grades, personality)
- When the team works out
- How important attendance and timeliness are
- The intensity of practices
- The attitude after winning or losing
- Team values
- Team captains
- Discipline

Perhaps the most important thing a coach controls is the overall tone of their team. Tone encompasses everything from how players treat each other to when, and to what degree, discipline is handed out. Imagine a new head coach of a basketball team giving their first speech to the team. Rules are outlined, and it is made known that if any of the rules are broken there will be clear consequences. A first offense means being benched for one half. A second offense means being benched for a full game. A third offense means being kicked off the team. This team's singular focus will be winning a championship, and that means being there for each other. Breaking the rules lets everyone know that you prioritize yourself over the team, and that won't fly.

Practices start, and the star player, a senior, is living up to all the hype. The effort is unmatched, and the rest of the team is following in the footsteps of the best player. Things are looking positive heading into their first game. On the day of their final preseason practice, the star player shows up two minutes late. The excuse: The alarm didn't go off. Coach has a tough decision to make. The rules were laid out, and being late means a player is benched for a half.

In that moment, the coach will set the tone for the rest of the season. If the offense is forgiven without penalty, then all credibility is lost and nobody will fear discipline. Additionally, it is obvious that talent supersedes team, and resentment for that player will set in.

The coach follows through, and the star player is benched for the first half of the first game. The team loses by 15 points, and every parent is questioning the decision to bench the best player on the team for being two minutes late for a practice. Making matters worse, the player is livid and threatens to quit.

Three weeks go by, and everything seemingly returns to normal. Then, the same player shows up ten minutes late to a film session. This time the excuse is that they were studying and lost track of time. Once again, the coach has a difficult decision to make. The team's opponent is the top-ranked team, and now they should be without their best player for the entire game. The coach decides to call a team meeting where it is once again made clear that it is team above all else. This means that their star player will not be benched for being late this time. The upcoming game is too important, and winning is top priority.

On game night, something seems off within the team. The vibe is awkward and the effort on the court is lacking at best. They get blown out for their second loss of the season. Over the course of the next few weeks, it only gets worse. Multiple players continually show up late, and there is bickering amongst the players. Looking back, the coach questions the decision to not sit the star player. They lost anyway, and now it seems as though the team is drifting apart.

These situations are the ones that make being a leader challenging. The best ones know that they are only as good as their word, and they are comfortable with making difficult decisions. Not benching the star player wasn't doing what was best for the team. It was a selfish decision that prioritized winning above all else. What would've been best for the team was to create a culture in which accountability, self-discipline, and dedication to one's teammates mattered above all else. That single decision changed the entire tone of the team, and that will now be harder to reverse.

## Team captain and teammates

Being the leader of a team in a captain role is much different from being a coach. Players are not friends or peers with their coaches. They are, however, both peers and friends with team captains. Additionally, players are going to spend significantly more time with each other than they will with their coaches. As discussed previously, your character reflects the character of the few people you spend the most time with. Therefore, the captain of a team has the ability to influence other players on an entirely different level than the coaches can.

Look again at the example about the star player who was late to practice from the perspective of that player. Let's say this player is also the captain. The captain could respond in one of two ways: Expressing anger, which is detrimental to the team, or taking on the problem in a positive way. As captain of the team, the star player should have addressed the team after the game. That player should have taken responsibility for letting down the team and renewed the commitment to the other players. Moving forward, anytime someone blames the coach for the loss, the captain should shoulder the blame and take responsibility. (A quality coach would also accept responsibility for not having the rest of the team ready to play up to a level needed to win.)

A captain must lead by example. Being a captain is like being an older brother or sister. Younger siblings look up to the older ones and do as they do without thought. There is an enormous amount of responsibility that comes with that. Remember, every player has their role on a team. Not everybody is made to be the captain. If you have what it takes to be a leader, embrace the role and know that you will be held to the highest of standards.

## Business owner and employees

Nobody will care about a business as much as the owner does. No matter how incredible the employee is, it is nearly impossible to care about something as much as the person who owns it. The owner has the risk and the most to lose. They are on the hook for all debt and, if the business fails, they will lose significantly more than any employee. On the other hand, they are also directly responsible for the success of their employees. I take a lot of pride in developing my staff and know that their success lies in my ability to teach them.

There are three simple rules every business owner should follow to give them the best chance at success:

1. Never ask your employees to do anything you aren't willing to do yourself.
2. Never stop learning and growing.
3. Genuinely care about your employees and their success.

A business owner has nobody to blame for their success, or lack thereof, but themself. The owner controls who they hire and how they build their team. The best employees aren't found, they are developed. Get rid of the ones who don't have the best interest of the company in mind. Culture starts at the top and trickles down. A business owner is a parent, teacher, coach, and captain.

## FINAL THOUGHTS

Leaders own their actions. Hold yourself accountable for everything you do. You, and you alone, are responsible for your actions. Stop passing blame to others. Leaders shoulder the blame for those around them and take personal responsibility for the success of their teams.

## REFLECTION

1. Name a situation when owning your actions would've allowed for growth.
2. What common characteristics do the best leaders in your life have?
3. Have you ever been in a leadership role and accepted responsibility for others?

CHAPTER 8

# MAKE AN IMPACT

Merriam-Webster Dictionary defines "impact" as "the force of impression of one thing on another: a significant or major effect."

When I decided to open a gym, my mission was to positively impact as many lives as possible through health and fitness. Those are things I have always been passionate about. However, passion without purpose does not guarantee success. There needed to be something more than just passion. Every decision made was done with intention and focus. The intent was to impact as many lives as possible, and the focus was on how to do so in a positive way. I knew that if I did those things, the rest would take care of itself.

I believe luck is a byproduct of hard work. Aside from winning the lottery, good things come to those who work relentlessly for them. From Day One I have done everything I could to build a community within our gym. I believe that prioritizing people is what has led to our success. If you were to ask any of our members what makes the gym so special, they wouldn't say the workouts or the facility; they would say it is the people. It's the coaching staff and the incredible relationships forged within our community that sets us apart.

Along with prioritizing people, there are three things that have contributed to building our community above all else.

## Never missing a call

While it drives my wife crazy at times, having my personal cell phone as our business phone has been invaluable. It gives me the ability to answer every phone call and respond to every message right away.

Early on, I couldn't afford to miss a phone call. Every call was a potential gym member. When you're trying to grow a small business, every lead is significant. A little time spent to make a connection, break down walls, and make someone laugh could almost always get a person to walk through our doors. Still today, I never want to miss those opportunities. If I answer a call immediately, I will get to talk to someone. However, if I choose not to answer, that missed call is probably a missed opportunity. Most of the time a caller doesn't leave a message, and if I return the call, either they won't answer or won't return my call.

I have listened to many experts who say that it is toxic to constantly live by your phone like I do. I don't see it that way. For the most part, my phone doesn't ring after 7 p.m. or on the weekends. I might get a total of 15 calls over the course of a week at those times. I think accepting those calls and messages has made a significant difference in the growth of our business. More than that, they provide a constant connection with our gym community that you won't find in many places. This is just one more way I choose to put people first.

## Taking advantage of every opportunity

Even the most incredible things begin with just the seed of an idea. A giant sequoia tree can grow to over 300 feet tall and weigh more than 2 million pounds, but it too started with a single seed.

In the case of our gym, our annual Athlete Development Camp is the single coolest thing we do for kids each year, and it keeps growing. This camp traces its roots to one conversation about our original speed and agility camps — running down gravel roads — in 2013.

I grew up playing baseball, and it is still my favorite sport.

When traveling baseball was starting to gain traction in town, I saw an opportunity to work with kids who wanted to go above and beyond with their training. I approached a parent involved in the program about getting baseball kids into a speed and agility camp at our gym. He took a leap of faith and helped me get more than 50 kids involved in our first camp. The success of that camp led to the development of an official youth program at our gym. Additionally, from that initial seed conversation with a parent, a friendship and business relationship developed. Over the years, he and I have served on a youth baseball board together, partnered on nutrition challenges, and have opened a nutrition office at our local hospital where he works. If I never would've approached him about working with his teams, things could look much different for our gym all around. That is another example of why it is so important to take advantage of every opportunity.

As our youth program continued to grow, a large number of kids spent extensive amounts of time in the gym. They would show up at 6 a.m. and come back again after school. They were hungry for more, and I felt an obligation to feed that hunger. I wanted to create something for the kids who had a desire to go beyond the ordinary. I wanted to create something for the elite — not necessarily elite from the standpoint of being physically gifted, but elite in mindset and work ethic.

In 2017, we hosted just over 20 kids in our very first Athlete Development Camp. In this one-week camp, we aim to give kids an inside look at what it really takes to be successful at the next level. Although we center our training on sports, this camp is as much about building character as it is progressing athletically. In 2022, 100 kids attended camp. Today, it takes a small army of coaches, a group of dedicated partners, and many, many hours of planning to run this camp. Through that work, positive relationships have grown with our partners, their parents, and the kids.

I knew we had created something special when I began to receive messages of gratitude from parents with kids involved in the camp. Nearly every one of them spoke of a noticeable difference in the confidence of their children. The conversations weren't about athletic ability, running faster, or jumping higher. Instead, they talked about the changes they saw in the way their kids carried themselves in and out of sports. Some were very emotional in the way they described how our gym has impacted their family. That kind of feedback is why I love what I do and why I will always continue to pour my heart and soul into all that we do.

## Making everything fun

To get the most out of anything you do, you need to genuinely enjoy doing it. Sure, you can grind through things, but passion is what drives you to go above and beyond. When you love something or someone, you will naturally do more for that thing or person. My wife and I are wired very differently. I wake up like a ball of fire at 3:30 a.m., ready to attack the day. I drive her bonkers when I come back home at 7 a.m. to see her and the kids. She often tells me she doesn't know how I do it. My answer is always the same: I love what I do. It's so much fun, and there are so many incredible things I'm working on, that I can't help but be excited all the time!

Very rarely will you see me without a smile on my face. Yes, I get tired. Yes, I have rough days. Yes, I worry about things from time to time. However, I always bring energy to everything I do. I am a big believer in the saying "Anything worth doing, is worth doing right." You are going to spend the same amount of time doing a task whether you like it or not. With that in mind, choosing to make tasks fun will change your mindset and make them go by faster. For example, odds are you don't really enjoy cleaning the house, doing chores, or homework. But perhaps if you listen to music while doing those things, they become more tolerable. For many people, that one little trick of listening to music can make any monotonous task better.

Negative thoughts and words have a direct effect on your attitude. Thinking to yourself how much you hate doing something won't make it any better, and saying you hate it out loud will only make it worse. Probably no mundane or routine tasks

*Becoming Elite*

are at the top of your list of how you would choose to spend your time. However, they need to be done, so your mindset when completing them is important. Saying things out loud in a certain way makes a difference. For example, say, "I'm going to get an A on this project!" instead of saying, "Homework sucks." Or, tell yourself, "Clean clothes smell so fresh!" rather than "I hate doing laundry."

It can be easy to let one thing ruin your day if your thoughts and words surrounding it are negative. Instead, focus on the positive outcomes of completing tasks. Look at everything you do as something positive accomplished. It's a good feeling to check things off your list, so throw some music on, smile, and get after it!

One of the easiest ways to make a positive impact on someone is to make them laugh. Others will be drawn to you if you make them smile. We choose our friends based on who we have fun with, and fun means laughter. Tell jokes. High five and fist bump people. Bring energy to the things you do. Light up a room. Be someone who others want to be around.

### Defining your legacy

The greatest part about a legacy is that you get to define it. You determine if and how you will be remembered by the impact you make on others. Why should you care about how people remember you? The answer to that question will tell you all you need to know about yourself and what you will accomplish in life. If everything you do in life is self-centered and internally focused, you will not leave a legacy at all. However, if you are selfless and make it a point to change the lives of those around you, your legacy will be one of greatness.

If you are the star quarterback of your high school football team, you may think your legacy will be defined by that role. However, what matters more than your status as quarterback is how you treat your teammates, coaches, and classmates. As the face of your team, you are given a platform from which to do things for others. Naturally, your voice will be heard above others. Use that as an opportunity to positively impact those around you. Let your play on the field speak for itself. If you want to leave a legacy, make your teammates better. Always encourage them and never tear them down. Deflect the spotlight from yourself and give credit to those around you. Respect your coaches and give everything you have in the weight room and on the field. Be the first to show up and the last to leave, every day. When you walk down the hall, high five the kid who gets bullied and stand up for him. Be a leader in the classroom as much as you are on the field.

If you are a successful business owner, you might think your legacy will be defined by how much money you make and how big your business grows. Instead, your legacy will be defined by how you take care of your employees and what you give to your community. Take the time to educate and develop your employees. Be a friend, not just a boss. If you have the means to do so, give back to your community. Take care of those who are less fortunate than you. Donate to your local schools, provide resources for charities to do their work, and make sure that your name is synonymous with giving.

If you are a parent, it can be easy to think you need to give everything to your kids. While providing opportunities for your children is important, they will remember you for the love you show them and the time you spend with them. What matters is the type of people your kids grow up to be. Your legacy is built within your children. Teach them to be selfless, caring, driven individuals. Your job is to set them up for success, not hand it to them.

When deciding how to live your life, ask yourself one question: "When people think of me, what are the three words they would use to describe me?"

### Wealthy, driven, and successful — or fun, caring, and selfless

There is absolutely nothing wrong with being wealthy, driven, and successful. The key is to get there by being fun, caring, and selfless. How you do things matters as much as what you do. That is how you make an impact and that is how you leave a legacy.

## FINAL THOUGHTS

Do everything with intent and purpose. Be unforgettable and an inspiration to others. You will be remembered for how you treat people and the lives you impact. A single drop creates a far-reaching ripple. When you believe in something, be relentless in your pursuit of that dream.

## REFLECTION

1. What kind of impact do you have on others?
2. How can you change a task you don't like to make it better?
3. What are three words people would use to describe you? Do those words align with the legacy you want to leave?

CHAPTER 9

# LIFE HACKS

There is one very specific time that made me realize the way a person dresses matters. When I was 18 years old, I got a job selling vacuum cleaners. I was good with people, and sales came easy to me. Within a few months, I became one of the leading salespeople in the country, and I worked my way up the ranks quickly. I earned cash bonuses, vacations, and was even promoted to a management position within a year. My new role as manager was to interview, hire, and train all employees. There was a very high turnover rate, so I was constantly grinding to keep people coming in the doors. I did well and the business grew. On a typical day, I would wear slacks, a dress shirt, and a tie to work. I was very young, so making an appropriate first impression on potential hires mattered.

One day, for reasons I can't remember, I decided to show up to work in khaki shorts, a Hawaiian button-up shirt, and sandals. That was a mistake. My boss had a bad temper, and I set him off when he saw me. I was in the front room with coworkers, hanging out before our morning meeting. He came out to start the meeting and, without hesitation, his face turned deep red and he told me to get into his office. For the next 10 minutes, I took the biggest butt-chewing of my life. Every person in the building could hear exactly what was going on. He was screaming uncontrollably which caused him to spit as he talked. He threw things off his desk, and every other word was a swear word. I remember these words: "Who do you think you are? Are you on vacation?" There were some other choice words thrown in there, but those two sentences are burned in my memory. From that day forward, I always wore a shirt and tie.

Perhaps he didn't handle things the way I would have, but it worked. He was right. The first impression every person got of his business was me. I was the first face they saw. For the first week, I was the only person they talked to. By changing my clothes, I went from being a young business professional to a college kid on spring break.

The lesson I learned that day carried over into my professional life moving forward. As I transitioned into selling real estate, I knew how to look the part. As a gym owner, our staff all has matching shirts, and we wear them whenever we are coaching. Baggy sweatpants and hooded sweatshirts simply aren't worn. I want our members to see and recognize us as professional coaches and not just other people working out.

Pro sports teams have matching uniforms. Players are expected to keep jerseys tucked in. You never see grass stains, holes, or dirty uniforms when a game starts. Image matters, and the way a person dresses says a lot without saying anything at all. Do not confuse this with being materialistic. You don't have to wear the most expensive name-brand clothes. You need to wear clean clothes, keep them wrinkle free, and dress appropriately for the occasion.

There are several things that I wish I had been taught growing up. Not only that, but I should've paid better attention and I wouldn't have missed opportunities. I have developed a list of eight rules to live by, or life hacks, that will benefit you in a variety of ways.

Dressing nicely is one of three that reference how to take care of your body and live your life. The other five tackle the subject of finances. Together, they provide a template for success.

### Prioritize your health.

You only get one body for the entirety of your life, so take care of it. Treat your body as if it is a car, and you only get to drive that one car forever. Elite athletes are Corvettes and Lamborghinis. The world's strongest men are military tanks. Marathon runners are hybrid cars that get 1,000 miles per tank of gas. Some people are minivans, and others are semi-trucks. You don't get to pick the body you're born with, but each type of body has a role and a use.

If you knew going in that the first car you ever drove would be the only one you'd have for the rest of your life, would you treat it differently? I know I would have.

My first car was a 1996 Pontiac Grand Am. It was red and packed a punch for a four-cylinder engine. I hot-rodded the heck out of that thing. I would pull the emergency brake, spin cookies, and tear around with my friends. I was an idiot. I cleaned it out and washed it from time to time, but I definitely didn't keep it spotless. I changed the oil when it was convenient and didn't understand the importance of rotating the tires. I also ran it out of gas a handful of times. There is no way that car would've lasted 20 years the way I took care of it.

I currently drive a 2016 Ford F-150. This is the nicest vehicle I've ever owned, and I take very good care of it. I learned my lesson after that first car — and grew up a little bit, too.

Just like with cars, most people don't understand why and how they should take care of their bodies until it's too late. According to the CDC and World Health Organization, heart disease is the leading cause of death in the world. Additionally, obesity rates are at an all-time high and continue to climb. Nine out of ten of the leading causes of death can all be made worse by being overweight or obese (this excludes neonatal deaths).

Don't wait for your doctor to tell you to get healthy. Start immediately. Find some type of fitness activity you enjoy, and do it with people you like spending time with. People are much more likely to stick with a fitness program if they are doing it with friends. Very few people can grind by themselves for years on end.

Pay attention to the fuel you put into your body. There is no secret or magic key. Stay away from processed foods and those high in fat and sugar. Keep nutrition simple. Eat to feel satiated, but never stuffed. The more active you are, the more fuel you need. Drink water. Take care of your body. You only get one.

## Have a plan.

I've heard numerous motivational speakers and watched dozens of videos that talk about knowing your "why." Having a reason to be motivated and a purpose for relentlessly pursuing a goal isn't a bad thing. It can provide fuel for your fire when you feel like quitting, and it keeps you pushing forward. However, I would argue that it's not the goal or the "why" that matters as much as the "how." Goals without a plan will never be met and a day with no agenda will be wasted.

There is a clear order of operations when it comes to executing goals.

1. Define a goal.
2. Understand why.
3. Develop a plan with clear objectives and tasks.

Start by figuring out exactly what you want to do. Then, write it down. Make your goal clear cut. For example, don't just say you want to be successful. Define what success means to you. Maybe it's graduating high school with a 4.0 GPA. Maybe it's getting a scholarship to play college sports. Maybe success, as a parent, means eating dinner with your family every night. Don't make your goal vague — to get better grades, to play college sports if you can, or to be home more. Be specific. Define exactly what you want to do. A vague goal will not paint a clear picture.

Next, understand why you are doing something. There needs to be purpose behind your goals. Why do you want a 4.0 GPA? You need that GPA to get into the college of your choice. Why do you want to get a scholarship to play college sports? A scholarship would mean you can afford to attend school and be able to concentrate on sports and classes without having to work or take out loans to pay for college. Eating dinner every night with your family will provide you time to spend with your kids. Maybe when you were a kid, your family never gathered around the dinner table together, and you want to change that for your own family.

Finally, put together a plan of action. How are you going to make sure you are successful in reaching your goals? Seek out advice, and write down your plan.

My plan for a 4.0 GPA:

1. Study for no less than 2 hours each night and read a book with extra time.
2. Turn off my phone by 9 p.m. each night, so I get quality sleep.
3. Meet with my math tutor twice a week.
4. No extracurricular activities unless my homework is finished.
5. Work out at 5 a.m. daily so my nights are free.

My plan to get a basketball scholarship:

1. Get my homework done ASAP.
2. Shoot 100 free throws each night.
3. Run 1 mile every day.
4. Work out at 5 a.m. daily.
5. Write down every workout in a journal.
6. Make a highlight video of games for recruiting.
7. Make the all-state traveling team this summer.
8. Work with my private coach three times a week.

My plan to eat dinner each night with my family:

1. Work out every morning before work.
2. Prep my lunch and take it to work, so I don't have to leave the office to eat.
3. Respond to my final email at 4 p.m. each day.
4. Write myself a list of tasks for the next day.
5. Leave work no later than 5:30 p.m. every day.
6. Do computer work from 6 a.m. to 8 a.m. on Saturdays.

Making a plan and committing it to paper will give you accountability and make your days flow smoothly. In the previous examples, there are lists of objectives to complete to reach the desired goal. Each of those objectives could be broken down further with specific tasks. Your plan should be as detailed as possible.

Taking a look at how sports work provides a template for making a plan to attain a goal. For example, a goal of winning a state championship is great, but how will a team accomplish that? The simplest way is to start with the end goal in mind and work backwards. A coach may develop a plan that looks like this:

Goal: Win the state championship.

9. Make it to the state playoffs.
8. Win districts.
7. Win subdistricts.
6. Every player achieves a GPA of 3.0 or higher.
5. Nobody misses more than three days of summer weights.
4. Nobody is late to practice.
3. Everybody controls effort by giving 100% — no excuses.
2. Build relationships with each other off the court/field.
1. Be positive through everything we do and never put another teammate down.

By starting with the end goal, you are able to look at things from the perspective of "If I want to accomplish that, then I need to do this." Another way to go about making a plan is to write each of your steps down on a separate piece of paper. Then, organize your thoughts by moving the pieces around into the correct order. You may know you want to win a district title, and your team will adopt a "no excuses" mindset, but what comes before, after, and between those things? Write steps down as you think of them and worry about the order afterwards.

As important as it is to keep the big-picture plan in mind, the day-to-day tasks must not be overlooked. A team of people can all be working toward the same goal, but individuals will have different tasks to accomplish each day. My employees and I all have the same goal of making our gym as successful as we can. We know our roles, and some things are set in stone. However, there is also a lot of variability in our individual schedules, so each of us has a different daily plan. I do three things that make my life much easier and keep my days running smoothly:

1. Keep a planner with my schedule.
2. Have a list of tasks that are done consistently.
3. Each night, text myself a next-day list of things to accomplish.

*Becoming Elite*

The planner I keep is a Google Drive spreadsheet with four weekly sheets. Each week is broken into seven days, and those days are broken into half-hour cells. My days start at 4 a.m. and run until 7 p.m. I am able to prefill time slots with things such as the classes I coach and personal training clients. I fill in the remaining times as I go. The advantage to using the Google Drive document is I am able to edit it from my phone anytime I am not by my computer. I can also share this document with my wife or anyone else who needs to know my schedule.

I also have a list of daily tasks that I keep. This list is constantly evolving as new projects come up and my business grows. Right now, here is what that list looks like:

1. Check emails morning, noon, and evening.
2. Social media post for gym and nutrition.
3. Post in social media groups.
4. Email nutrition clients.
5. Review tomorrow's workout.
6. Send nightly email to gym members.

This list is similar to a list of chores to be done on a daily basis. I like to knock out as many of these tasks early in the day as possible. Doing so allows me to concentrate on other projects that need my attention. Additionally, there are many unforeseen things that pop up throughout the day. Procrastinating on the routine tasks may lead to not getting everything done.

The final thing I do on a nightly basis is send myself an email with a list of things to accomplish the next day. I have a wide variety of projects going all the time, and I receive numerous text messages and phone calls about things that need taken care of. Here is an example of one of those lists:

1. Put real estate sign in client's yard.
2. Pick up real estate sign in client's yard.
3. Call an organization about partnering on fitness event.
4. Make spreadsheet of all nutrition clients.
5. Design Christmas party invitation.

Organize your life in whatever way works for you. Prioritize the tasks that need done each day, and then make a plan to accomplish larger projects. Be prepared to stay flexible because you will certainly have things pop up you hadn't planned to do.

Even the best-made plans fail. In any sports event, there can only be one winning team or individual. You can still be successful without accomplishing the goal you set. Don't forget to learn along the way. Fall in love with the process, and give as much to each moment as you do to the end goal itself. When it's all over, the habits you developed, the memories you made, and the fun you had will remain.

## Money

Money is definitely not the key to happiness. However, being financially responsible at a young age can open doors for you later in life. If I had the knowledge 15 years ago that I do now, I would be in a much different financial position today. In my experience, there are four things you can do to set yourself up for success with money. It's never too late to start, but the sooner you do, the better off you will be.

1. Live below your means.
2. Don't spend to impress.
3. Save your money.
4. Invest your money and understand the value of compound interest.

Living below your means is the only way you will ever be financially free. At the most basic level, this means spending less than you earn. However, there needs to be a more definitive plan of action if you want to be successful with saving and investing money. For example, if you earn $2,500 each month and spend $2,490 each month, you are technically spending less than you earn. That $10 left over at the end of each month won't get you very far, though. On the other hand, spending only $1,500 per month will leave you with $1,000 to save and invest.

Cut back as much spending as possible to get ahead of the game with your money. Avoid debt, other than a house, whenever possible. Avoid credit cards. Don't finance expensive vehicles. Don't go out to eat or buy $7 coffees when you can prep food and drinks at home. Realize you don't need name-brand clothes all the time. The less you spend in the moment will allow you to spend exponentially more down the road.

Every time you are about to spend money, ask yourself if you are doing it for you or for someone else. Why do you want to buy the expensive sports car? Any decent car will get you from Point A to Point B. Why do you need fancy clothes and name-brand everything? Your friends should like you for the person you are, not for the items you possess. Speaking from experience, I can assure you that all the material things you think matter now are not really that important.

To avoid debt, you need to use cash to pay for things. Use cash to pay for a date-night meal with your spouse, tickets to a concert or sporting event with friends, or a vehicle. If you don't have the money in cash, make other plans. Cook dinner together and eat at home. Sit on the patio and listen to music with your friends. Watch the big game on TV. Ride your bike, walk, or carpool to go places. Set some cash aside as emergency money, too. When the unexpected happens, having cash to pay those expenses will eliminate some of the stress.

Investing money and understanding the value of compound interest are real game changers. Inflation is real, and a dollar will go much farther today than it will 20 years from now. I remember gas being just over $1 per gallon when I started driving. Now gas costs nearly four times that. Median home prices are more than double what they were 20 years ago. One dollar 20 years ago is still a dollar today, but it simply won't buy as much. Making your money work for you by earning interest is the key.

Historically, the average rate of return for the Standard and Poor's 500 stock market index is about 10%. Look at the following numbers to see how compound interest works with that same 10% rate of return:

| Monthly Contribution | Years | Total Money | Your Contributions | Total Interest Earned |
|---|---|---|---|---|
| $50 | 10 | $10,072.88 | $6,000 | $4,072.88 |
| $50 | 20 | $36,199.34 | $12,000 | $24,199.34 (2x) |
| $50 | 30 | $103,964.64 | $18,000 | $85,964.64 (5x) |
| $50 | 40 | $279,730.37 | $24,000 | $255,730.37 (10x) |
| $200 | 10 | $40,291.52 | $24,000 | $16,291.52 |
| $200 | 20 | $144,797.35 | $48,000 | $96,797.35 |
| $200 | 30 | $415,858.54 | $72,000 | $343,858.54 |
| $200 | 40 | $1,118,921.48 | $96,000 | $1,022,921.48 |
| $500 | 10 | $100,728.80 | $60,000 | $40,728.80 |
| $500 | 20 | $361,993.36 | $120,000 | $241,993.36 |
| $500 | 30 | $1,039,646.36 | $180,000 | $859,646.36 |
| $500 | 40 | $2,797,303.70 | $240,000 | $2,557,303.70 |

The longer you hold an investment, the more it pays off. After 20 years, you will have earned double the money you invested from interest. However, wait another 20 years and that number grows to over 10 times the amount you invested! The key is to invest early, and as much as you can, after being debt free. Start with a Roth IRA as the gains are tax free when you go to withdraw from it later in life (current age 59½). As your income grows, contribute more and more to your investments and diversify your portfolio.

With the help of some good friends and investors, I was finally able to purchase the real property that our gym is affixed to in 2020. The plan was to buy it much earlier, but things don't always go according to plan. My business partner walked out the day we opened our current facility in 2013. His role in our business plan was half of the income to the gym. I knew going in that I was going to rent for a couple years, but owning the property was supposed to happen relatively soon. If I would've saved and invested my money the right way, I would have the property nearly paid for by now.

I made some very poor financial decisions when I was younger. I spent money as quickly as I earned it and used credit cards at will. Looking back, if I'd known then what I know now, I would have done things much differently. Beginning at the age of 18, I would've saved every penny possible to have $10,000 in savings within a year. At 19 years old, I would've begun investing $400 per month in a Roth IRA (annual limits were lower then). I also would have invested $500 per month in a brokerage account with my money in the S&P 500. As my income grew, I would have invested more money into the brokerage account and added to savings, as well. I know that I could've worked very hard and had at least $1,500 per month to save and invest, if not more. Under that system, by 2013, at the age of 29, I could've purchased our gym with one investor contributing 10%.

Additionally, rent was $6,000 per month for nearly seven years, totaling $504,000. None of that rent paid went towards equity in a property that I owned.

With those decisions instead of the ones I made, here is where I would be currently:

Today: 37 years old (started at age 19) — Roth IRA

| Monthly Contribution | Years | Total Money | Your Contributions | Total Interest Earned |
|---|---|---|---|---|
| $400 | 18 | $228,735.24 | $86,400 | $142,335.24 |

Under this scenario, if I were to continue to invest $500 per month for another 23 years, until the age of 60, my Roth IRA would look like this:

60 years old — Roth IRA

| Monthly Contribution | Years | Total Money | Your Contributions | Total Interest Earned |
|---|---|---|---|---|
| $500 | 23 | $2,546,920.62 | $224,400 | $2,180,185.38 |

And if I had started a brokerage account at age 19, that account would grow as well:

24 years old (started at age 19) — Brokerage Account

| Monthly Contribution | Years | Total Money | Your Contributions | Total Interest Earned |
|---|---|---|---|---|
| $500 | 5 | $38,280.62 | $30,000 | $8,280.62 |

If I'd continued to invest $1,000/mo for another five years, until the age of 29, my brokerage account would look like this:

29 years old — Brokerage Account

| Monthly Contribution | Years | Total Money | Your Contributions | Total Interest Earned |
|---|---|---|---|---|
| $1,000 | 5 | $138,212.55 | $60,000 | $39,931.93 |

The total property cost in 2013 was $1,000,000. With a 10% ($100,000) investment from one investor, we would've been able to purchase the property with a 20% ($200,000) down payment and I would've had $38,212.55 left in my brokerage account. Financing $800,000 for 15 years at a 5% interest rate, equals a payment of $6,326.35. Fast forward eight years and I would be more than halfway to owning a piece of real estate currently valued at nearly $1. 5 million. At the age of 44, my business would be completely debt free and worth even more than it is today!

Under this scenario, if I were to continue to invest $1,000 per month in my brokerage account (starting with $38,212.55) for another 30 years, until the age of 59, my brokerage account would look like this:

| Monthly Contribution | Years | Total Money | Your Contributions | Total Interest Earned |
|---|---|---|---|---|
| $1,000 | 30 | $2,729,629.47 | $420,000 | $2,331,416.92 |

At the age of 60, my portfolio would look like this:

| Gym Property | Roth IRA | Brokerage Account | Total |
|---|---|---|---|
| $1,500,000 | $2,546,920.62 | $2,729,629.47 | $6,776,550.09 |

Even though it took me a while to figure out the right way to save and invest my money, I'm glad I now know what to do. My wife and I are aggressively saving and investing to catch up. Her job offers a company match 401(k) up to 6% and, other than our house, we are debt free. We max out our Roth IRAs and are investing for our kids' college. We just opened a brokerage account and are doing our very best to set ourselves up for the future.

I am not a financial advisor, but I have done my research and figured out what works for me and my family. I follow financial people such as Dave Ramsey and The Money Guys on YouTube. There is no one-size-fits-all plan. I encourage you to seek out professionals and learn from those who are where you want to be financially. Do not take financial advice from anyone who isn't successful themselves. Never forget, true happiness does not lie in money itself. However, being financially adept is another tool in your belt that will help you achieve your personal goals for success.

*Becoming Elite*

## Tip well.

If a person does an exceptional job, tip appropriately. It doesn't matter what the service is, if a person earns it, tip well. If that person goes above and beyond, tip very well. Being in a relationship-driven business, I understand how difficult it can be to put a smile on your face all the time. We all have bad days and things going on in our lives that will bring us down from time to time. For that reason, put yourself in someone else's shoes when considering how to tip.

For example, if you are out to eat and your server is quiet and does an average job, you should still tip. You never know what happened before you sat down to eat. Maybe the last table your server had was full of obnoxious people who made life miserable for an hour. Maybe your server has three kids at home, takes care of a parent in poor health, and works 70 hours a week to make ends meet. Maybe your server just lost a loved one or had a terrible fight with his or her spouse. If that person provided you with excellent service and a positive attitude, you should tip extremely well. Someone can still be going through all those things and give excellent service. They should be rewarded for doing so. Tipping well encourages someone to keep working hard, can brighten a day, and will also give you a sense of satisfaction.

## Get quality sleep.

The first step to getting quality sleep is turning off your TV and putting down your phone at a decent time. Social media, playing video games, and watching TV all cause your brain to release dopamine. That hit of dopamine means you get a positive, euphoric feeling when you get "likes" on social media, win a game, or watch your favorite TV show. Over time, this trains your brain to crave those things and you become addicted. Start by breaking that habit. Turn off all devices an hour before bed. Relax, spend time with family, or read. Allow your body to calm down and prep for sleep. Like warming up before a workout, you should cool down before sleep. Of course, you can just jump into a workout or crash into bed without preparation, but the quality of each will suffer.

Most studies show that your body needs at least eight hours of sleep each night to recover fully. However, sometimes life doesn't allow for that much time sleeping. This is when the quality matters more than the quantity. I am asleep by 9:30 p.m., and my alarm goes off at 3:30 a.m. most mornings. That equates to six hours of sleep, and I function extremely well on that amount. I also lead a healthy lifestyle, exercise daily, eat quality food 95% of the time, and very rarely drink alcohol. I have found that keeping my body in a routine makes a big difference. I work out first thing in the morning whenever possible, and I do not sleep in past 6 a.m. on the weekends.

The more you break down your body, the more sleep you will require. If you are an athlete who trains for hours each day, you will need more than five or six hours of sleep. Deep sleep is when your muscles recover the most as blood flow increases and growth hormone is released. Consider your goals when determining sleep requirements, bedtimes, and nightly habits. Additionally, if you sleep six to eight hours each night, you will sleep for at least one-fourth of your life. That means you need to make the absolute most of every minute you are awake. Quality sleep allows you to perform at the top of your game and maximize your potential.

### Master the basics.

There are several basic things everyone should know how to do on their own. While more could certainly be added to this list, here are four skills for self-sufficiency that everyone should be able to do. Mastering these skills will lay a foundation for independence and self-care.

1. Cooking
2. Cleaning
3. Laundry
4. Changing a tire

Bodybuilding was my first love in the world of fitness. Even though I own a CrossFit gym today, I still follow the sport of bodybuilding closely. It was that love that forced to me to learn how to cook healthy food. Trying to eat nearly 5,000 calories per day of the same boring food quickly grew old. Cooking became a passion of mine, and I enjoyed figuring out new ways to meal prep that provided a wide variety of foods and flavors. Not only did I learn how to cook, but I wrote my own meal plans and tracked my caloric intake. A decade of studying, watching cooking videos, and experimenting gave me the knowledge to help people with nutrition as part of my career. I even published a meal prep guide in 2020. Knowing how to cook quality food will allow you to eat healthily and enjoy the foods you consume.

Will Durant wrote, "We are what we repeatedly do. Excellence, then, is not an act, but a habit." Cleaning is perhaps more of a habit that is developed rather than a skill that is learned. The importance of keeping everything in your life clean cannot be understated. Start by looking inside your car. How does it look? How does it smell? Do you vacuum it out and wipe it down on a regular basis? Next, did you make your bed this morning? Are your clothes picked up off the floor? Are the dishes done, or do you leave them sitting in the sink for days at a time? When was the last time you cleaned your bathroom? The toilets?

From the first day our gym opened, it has been picked up and cleaned every night. The cleanliness has been one of the most consistent compliments I have received over the years. For the first five years we were open, I cleaned the gym and mopped the floors every night. Additionally, I would come in on the weekends for hours and do a deep cleaning of the equipment and all the hard-to-reach places.

There a number of reasons keeping a clean gym is important:

1. First impressions
2. Preventing the spread of disease and bacteria
3. Equipment longevity
4. Pride

Each morning, I walk in at 4 a.m. to a neatly organized, clean gym. I get a sense of accomplishment and pride seeing what I have worked so hard for. I know I wouldn't have that same feeling if the floors were dirty, equipment was scattered everywhere, and the gym smelled of sweat.

Creating self discipline is one of the values we teach at our

Athlete Development Camp. It starts with not hitting the snooze button and by making your bed each morning. That discipline is compounded by the habit of picking up after yourself and keeping things clean. Durant was correct in defining excellence as a habit and not a skill. The simple act of picking up after yourself lays a foundation for excellence.

Do your laundry! Learn how to use an iron. Learn which clothes can be washed together and at what temperature. I can't count the number of times that I have heard college kids talk about dropping off laundry at home for Mom to do for them. If you are wise enough to make your own decisions, you can do your own laundry.

Changing a tire is something we hope we never have to do. However, when that time inevitably comes, being able to do so will save you valuable time and money. The last thing anyone wants is to be stranded on the side of the road with a flat tire. That situation can be exacerbated by bad weather, no cell phone service, or a lack of traffic. If nobody is around to help, you will be completely reliant on your own ability to get back on the road. Changing or jumping a battery and checking fluid levels are other things to add to this list. Spend a couple hours practicing in your driveway. Someday, you will be thankful you did.

## FINAL THOUGHTS

Learn the basic skills you need in life. Do not become dependent on others. Invest your money and invest it early. The magic of compound interest is incredible.

## REFLECTION

1. When was a time you should have dressed to impress?
2. What are you doing to take care of your body?
3. Define a goal, understand why you have that goal, and write out a plan to reach it.
4. How do you handle your money? Are you setting yourself up for future financial success?
5. What are your sleep habits, and should you make adjustments?
6. Do you have the "four basics" mastered?

*Becoming Elite*

# FINAL THOUGHTS

### Chapter 1: 1 Life 1 Opportunity

You get one chance at life, and you have one opportunity to chase your dreams. Define your goals and make a plan to reach them. Decide the type of person you want to be, and stay true to yourself along the way. Accept failure as an opportunity for growth, and always dream big.

### Chapter 2: The Company You Keep

Choose your friends wisely. Your character reflects the character of the few people you spend the most time with. Surround yourself with people who are better than you; this is how you grow.

### Chapter 3: Act Elite

Act as though your loved ones are always watching. Do things that would make them proud. Stand out in a crowd. Walk with confidence and, when you shake someone's hand, look them in the eyes. Hold the door for others, and do the little things that matter, especially when nobody is looking.

### Chapter 4: Think, Then React

It is impossible to think clearly when upset. Wait 24 hours before you post anything on social media. Once it's out there, you can't take it back. Avoid impulse decisions and things that feel good in the moment. Keep your goals in mind, and make decisions based on what will help you reach them. Always listen, then think, and then react. Doing so in this order matters.

## Chapter 5: Control Your Effort

Give all your effort to anything you do. You cannot control the effort of others, and nobody can control yours. You are responsible for your success.

## Chapter 6: Attitude

Be positive. Find the good in every situation, and never complain, because doing so will change nothing. Your attitude will either hinder or facilitate your goals. Realize that you cannot control certain things, but you can control how you react to everything. Learn to take responsibility for your actions and your success. Nobody else will care as much as you do.

## Chapter 7: Own Your Actions

Leaders own their actions. Hold yourself accountable for everything you do. You, and you alone, are responsible for your actions. Stop passing blame to others. Leaders shoulder the blame for those around them and take personal responsibility for the success of their teams.

## Chapter 8: Make an Impact

Do everything with intent and purpose. Be unforgettable and an inspiration to others. You will be remembered for how you treat people and the lives you impact. A single drop creates a far-reaching ripple. When you believe in something, be relentless in your pursuit of that dream.

## Chapter 9: Life Hacks

Learn the basic skills you need in life. Do not become dependent on others. Invest your money and invest it early. The magic of compound interest is incredible.

ABOUT THE AUTHOR

# TREVOR BROWN

I am 38 years old at the time of this writing, and I'm a Nebraskan, born and raised. I outkicked my coverage when I married my beautiful wife, Jade. We are proud to be parents to the most amazing little girls in the world, Brynnlee and Kinsley.

I am the owner of Kearney CrossFit in Kearney, Nebraska, and the founder and head coach of BELITE Training and BELITE Nutrition. I started Kearney CrossFit in 2012 in my mom's garage. We moved in January 2013 to a 1,500-square-foot warehouse. Later that year, we built and moved into our current location, a 6,000-square-foot gym with a football-field-size training field out the back door. Our gym community of 200-plus members includes people from 7 years old to 70 years old.

Kearney CrossFit provided a solid foundation for our sub-businesses to grow.

BELITE Training started as a sport-specific training program for young athletes. Each year we ran speed and agility camps for kids, but we wanted to do something more for those looking to put in extra work in the gym. Our BELITE Athlete Development Camp is the single coolest thing I get to be a part of each year. Since starting it in 2017, BELITE Training has evolved into a full-service training program for young athletes. It is our mission to build good humans as much as elite athletes.

I am a go-getter, and I never slow down. I am up at 3:30 a.m. nearly every day and function well on six hours of sleep. I most the most of my time, taking advantage of every minute of every day. On top of being a dad and husband, I coach CrossFit classes, personally train clients, meet with nutrition clients, write programming for my online clients, and run the day-to-day operations of Kearney CrossFit, BELITE Training, BELITE Nutrition, and Level 4 Nutrition. Additionally, I hold a real estate license. Real estate provides me with a second income stream and is something I very much enjoy doing. The relationships I have built at the gym have enhanced my success in real estate.

I prioritize my own health and wellness. I work out an hour each day and track what I eat. Over the years, my focus has changed drastically from being an athlete and coach to being just a full-time coach. Coaching is my passion. I believe that when you are given a platform, you should positively impact as many lives as possible. Our gym has provided me with a platform, and I am going to use it to help change the lives of others.

I have a background in physique/bodybuilding-style training and baseball. I got started in CrossFit because of the carryover to sports. CrossFit is not for everyone, but a lot of the basic principles and practices can be applied to every type of training. I am here to help each of my clients reach their goals in whatever capacity is best for them individually. I see myself more as a life coach than just a fitness coach. What I do with my clients goes well beyond simply providing workouts and nutrition advice. I aim to change every aspect of my clients' lives for the better. A person's total health and wellness extends far beyond the walls of any gym.

After nearly two decades of experience and leading the lifestyle I preach, I have everything I need to help people reach their goals. However, I never want to stop learning. I constantly read books and watch videos from the most successful people in the world. I believe nothing can replace hard work and good habits. Quick fixes never last. Don't wait for the time to be right. Dig in, be willing to learn, give maximum effort to everything you do, and you will reach your goals!

*Becoming Elite*

# ACKNOWLEDGMENTS

Thank you to my incredible wife, Jade, for being by my side and having my back, always. Your efforts behind the scenes make our world go 'round. Without you, none of this would be possible.

Thank you to the people that make up our community at Kearney CrossFit. To all of you, from our members to our amazing BELITE Camp partners, thank you for making my job so much fun. You are the reason I get to do what I love, and you are the driving force behind all that we do.

Finally, thank you, Mom. It is because of your selflessness and unconditional support that I am where I am today.